Music for Your Child

A Complete Guide for Parents and Teachers

Music for Your Child

A Complete Guide for Parents and Teachers

Roberta Markel

Facts On File Publications
460 Park Avenue South
New York, N.Y. 10016

Music for Your Child
A Complete Guide for Parents and Teachers

Copyright © 1983 by Roberta Markel

Library of Congress Cataloging in Publication Data

Markel, Roberta.
  Music for your child.

  Rev. ed. of: Parents' and teachers' guide to music education. [1972]
    Includes index.
    1. Music—Instruction and study. I. Title.
MT1.M155 1983   780'.7'2   82-12066
ISBN 0-87196-754-5

Printed in the United States of America

10 9 8 7 6 5 4 3 2 1

Contents

Preface

Is my child talented? Should he take music lessons? How old should he be when he starts? What instrument should he play? How much does it cost? Is it really worth it?

These are some of the questions asked by parents who want to provide the best education for their children. But what is the *best music education* for a child? Which children should study music? What should they study? Where? When? And how?

This book attempts to answer these and many other questions that parents ask. Along with information and instruction, it will hopefully provide inspiration as well.

Musical skills are acquired in much the same way that a child learns his own language. First, a baby *hears* his parents talking; he *listens* to the language all around him. Then, one day he *imitates* it and begins to speak. His speech is very simple at first, but the more he hears and imitates the more complex it becomes. Then, as the child grows older he learns to *read* his language and to translate its symbols into sounds. Finally he learns to *write* his language and to put his own ideas into symbols for others to read and to share.

Music is a fundamental experience that belongs to everyone. Because it is a way to communicate ideas and emotions, it is a social art.

So, when we think of "music lessons" for our children, we shouldn't think just of the study of a particular instrument; we should consider the comprehensive study of the language as a means of expression and communication.

I hope this book will help parents and their children find ways to enjoy this universal language all their lives.

Acknowledgments

A number of people have contributed to the ideas found in this book beside the author. Some were teachers, others students and parents. I am especially grateful to the founder and director of the School of Music Education in New York City, where I taught for some eight years. Anne Holden is truly one of the most remarkable and important music educators I have ever encountered. Her ideas, her principles and practices have influenced me greatly in developing my own methods and in my teaching in general.

I am most grateful to Professor Lawrence Eisman of Queens College, who read the manuscript and made a number of valuable suggestions.

I would also like to offer a special salute to Gene and Kay North, who started me on my teaching career when I was just sixteen and who, several times, in the many years since, have advised me and encouraged me.

And last of all my very special gratitude to my husband, Bob, who helped in ways which helped most.

To Suzi and Peter

Music for Your Child

A Complete Guide
for Parents and Teachers

1

Taking Music Lessons

It is a rare parent who has not asked himself at one time or another, "I wonder if my child has any musical talent?"

Talent is actually not that hard to identify or define. We have all seen children with a certain natural ability, a special aptitude. And we know that talent also means the capacity to achieve or succeed.

There are several basic abilities we ordinarily associate with musical talent, such as outstanding physical aptitude for and dexterity on a particular instrument, or outstanding natural vocal ability. We can also immediately recognize an exceptional musical memory or an acutely sensitive musical ear. But there is a component—perhaps the most important component—which we don't really know how to identify. It distinguishes the "artist" from the technically proficient performer; it is the difference between the child from whom music seems to pour and the child who is very good at music. It has something to do with a natural emotional and aesthetic response to sound that is almost physical. Few people possess it in abundance. We do know that without it, and a generous supply of other critical elements, there would be no Beethovens, Stravinskys or Bernsteins.

While only a few will emerge as the great and

near-great in any age, we are all born with some music in us. It is unusual to find people with no musical talent; most of us have some natural ability and will respond to stimulation and education or exposure sufficiently for a satisfying musical experience. No one has to be labeled a "listener." Music is a performing art for everyone!

Before the child learns arithmetic do we ask, "Will he be another Einstein?" Why must we ask if the child is talented enough to be another Mozart before deciding whether musical training will be "worthwhile?" Music is a basic part of human knowledge and experience. It should be—in fact, it must be—a part of any comprehensive educational program for children. Every child has the right to explore and discover his abilities and then to develop them to the fullest. So, yes, of course your child, and every other child, should take music lessons.

What Is the Best Age for Starting?

There is no "proper" starting age for music instruction. Ideally, in a home where the parents enjoy music and are not inhibited in expressing themselves musically, the *informal* music education of a child begins on the day he comes home from the hospital.

Just as an infant hears speech, so he will hear singing, the playing of a stereo set or of live instruments. These sounds become a natural part of his world and are indelibly imprinted upon his ear and his senses. Music and music-making become associated with pleasure in this child's mind.

Someone sings to him from the time he is in the crib. He hears the piano played and is allowed to experiment with its sounds, first by banging on the keys and later in a more organized way, but always with gentle encouragement. The child discovers rhythm with his rattle and top, even with his spoon while eating. Children who are constantly urged into silence are not likely to develop a positive attitude toward making music later. But the child who is encouraged to explore sound—that of his own voice and those he can make with whatever lies about him—is fortunate. He is being trained then and there as a music maker; his home is his first concert hall.

Music in the home is one of the most important factors in determining the best starting age for "formal" music lessons for your child. In a home where there is no significant musical life, it is best to provide a vital musical experience outside at an early age. This should be a *group* experience and can begin when the child is two and-a-half or three years old. Many good music schools and private teachers offer appropriate group lessons for very young children. These classes in which the children are grouped chronologically, usually meet once or twice a week, for about a half hour or a little longer. They are very informal and allow each child to take what he or she can from the experience; much depends on the child's level of social, emotional and musical maturity. Incidentally, this type of class is a fine way to introduce a young child to a group experience before, or instead of, nursery school.

These classes should give the young child an opportunity to explore and experience the various elements of musical expression: rhythm, melody, harmony, dynamics and form. Naturally, there should be a good deal of singing, and no pressure to produce any specific technical advance. Try to avoid a group in which the singing is haphazard. Appropriate singing should include the kind of material that will help the child discover his vocal-auditory responses; imitation, singing high and low, singing loudly and softly, and so forth. Most of the child's responses, aside from singing, are through the use of the body and simple rhythm instruments. It is almost essential that the teacher of such a class either use a pianist with the ability to improvise, or be a pianist herself.

Every child can benefit from such an experience. For the child who has no musical life at home, it can be especially stimulating. This kind of class can continue as the child gets older; the lessons become more advanced in content and in what is expected of the students. The playing of a simple melody instrument, such as a tonette or a song flute, is often included in intermediate groups; and at a still older level, the instrument is a recorder. There is also the opportunity for children especially gifted in body movement to sense the possibilities in dance.

At What Age Should a Child Begin Study of an Instrument? Should the Lessons Be Private or in a Group?

Once again, there is no correct starting age for instrumental lessons. It depends on many factors and is very much an individual decision. However, there are certain generalities which can be useful as guidelines.

Most children do not possess enough *self*-discipline before the age of about eight years to make the formal study of an instrument a particularly satisfactory experience. Studying an instrument, in contrast to the type of group experience described above, makes very definite demands on the student not only in the lesson situation but also during the rest of the week. Success is impossible unless the student is mature enough to apply himself to organized and regular practice at home. If the student begins too young and is not yet *self-* disciplined enough to work at an assignment, he will not progress and will soon become discouraged and unhappy. There *are* ways a parent can help the child develop the skills of profitable and organized practicing (see Chapter 2).

Obviously, a student will receive more individual attention in a private lesson than in a group lesson. But there are certain advantages to *beginning* instrumental instruction in a group. The stimulation and motivation that come from learning with others cannot be overlooked. If the teacher is skillful, there can be healthy competition without unhealthy pressures. The study of an instrument becomes a social experience in which the child can share right from the start. This often provides the necessary motivation for the home practice that makes the experience successful. Students can share the mistakes and accomplishments of classmates; they are all "in the same boat." Often a pleasant feeling of comradeship develops, which adds to their interest. Also, the group lesson provides a built-in ensemble experience which should be part of good musical training.

Most good private teachers realize the need for ensemble playing and practicing. They will play duets with their students and arrange for their students to often get together in small groups. The student who learns the importance of his fellow players' contributions and who early in his musical life senses the special feelings one gets when perfectly "in tune" with the other players is experiencing some of the most joyous moments that life and music have to offer.

How Should You Choose a Music School or Private Teacher?

Most music schools have a catalogue describing the school's educational goals and basic approaches, specific courses, and usually the staff members and their credentials. In some cases, the reputation of a school is a byword in the community. Nevertheless you should check out a school in a variety of ways. One excellent source is the opinion of parents whose children have attended. You can discover rather quickly whether the school is interested in maintaining its own educational principles and standards or is one that will accommodate any parental whim in order to attract additional tuition.

Examine the catalogue and see if the course of study offered is comprehensive. In addition to private instruction on various instruments, does the school offer some kind of group experience? Are there classes in music theory, ear training, composition? Has the school developed performing groups in which your child can participate, such as choruses, glee clubs, orchestras, chamber music groups? Will the school provide for frequent informal solo and ensemble performances for *all* students? Since music is an art to be shared with others, only through much *informal* experience does the student learn to perform with confidence before an audience.

Check staff members' credentials for three things: their education and training background; their performing experience; their *teaching* experience. The latter is very important. Often a person can be an outstanding musician and performer but cannot teach. Although the reverse is possible, the good music teacher can usually do himself what he is teaching others to do.

Private music teachers are not licensed or certified unless they also teach in a public education system that requires it. Consequently, there is an enormous range in the abilities of the teachers available in most communities. Recommendations from parents and students whose opinions you respect can help. Sometimes the local music store can provide several names or at least confirm that so and so might be a good teacher for your child. The music teachers in the local public and private schools are also a source for either a good private teacher or a music school. Their opinions can be particularly significant if they are already familiar with your child in a learning situation and are aware of his individual needs. Often, of course, they either teach privately or at a music school and will already be known to you. Proceed as you would when "hiring" any other professional. Convenience is an asset; but what counts most is whether a teacher will be able to give your child the proper instruction. If possible, speak to more than one teacher. But make the final decision yourself. Your own instinct about what is right for your child is often a better guide than any professional opinion.

In choosing a teacher, keep in mind that some prefer to teach younger children and beginners; others do a better job with intermediate and advanced students who are at least ten or older. Also, consider the personality of the teacher. Some children work best and are happiest in a fairly formal, well-structured and disciplined atmosphere. Other children whose self-discipline is quite strong need a teacher who will help them relax, be more flexible and less self-demanding in their music. If the teacher is striving for concert-quality performance, this may create an unrealistic and discouraging goal for your child. The teacher who emphasizes music-making for personal satisfaction might work out better in terms of your child's advancement.

In your search for a private teacher, do not be embarrassed about asking for credentials and experience. If a teacher has them, he or she will be pleased to tell you. Also inquire about ensemble and solo performing opportunities. Most good private teachers have informal recitals once or twice a year. Many private teachers give group as well as individual lessons.

Where Should the Lessons Take Place?

If your child is attending a music school, this question is answered for you. Lessons take place at school and the parent *may not* be present except for special visiting days. The importance of this cannot be stressed enough. Many children cannot do their best work when a parent is in the room or even within earshot. Regardless of the fine relationship the parent and child might enjoy, the parent's presence at the lesson may create tensions which cannot help but inhibit learning and the establishment of a good student-teacher relationship.

If the child studies with a private teacher it is far more desirable for the student to go to the teacher's home or studio than for the teacher to come to the child's home. Do not let the convenience of a teacher coming to your home influence you unduly, *unless it is the only possible arrangement.* A music lesson in the living room, even if Mommy isn't there and cannot hear, is a situation filled with built-in distractions. The phone rings. The doorbell rings. A brother arrives home from school. There is the smell of something good coming from the kitchen. A friend yells to come out and play. However, if the student goes to the teacher's home or studio for the lesson, the environment is associated specifically with music; it becomes something special for your child and his fellow students alone.

How Long Should a Lesson Be?

The average weekly music lesson, either private or in a group, is about forty-five minutes. Some very young children, or those with particularly short concentration spans, can benefit from only a thirty-minute lesson. Students who are a bit more mature and on a more advanced level require a full hour lesson. It is rare that a lesson should be shorter than a half hour or longer than one hour. In a music school, the lesson periods are scheduled very tightly, with one student usually preceding and one immediately following your child's lesson. Hence, it is important that your child arrive a few minutes before his lesson so he is ready to start on time. If your child arrives late, time will be taken away from his lesson. A private teacher can sometimes be more flexible, but it is unreasonable to expect such accommodations. It is always polite and good sense to be on time.

Setting up the Business Relationship

Many people are embarrassed about discussing fees with professional people such as doctors and lawyers—and even music teachers. But you must re-

alize that you are hiring someone to perform a service, and to avoid unnecessary misunderstandings
later it is best that both parties be quite clear about
all the arrangements in advance.

How much should a lesson cost? There is as wide a
range of fees for music lessons as there is for a
doctor's examination. It depends on the standing
of the teacher within the profession. Teachers with
outstanding reputations as soloists or leading orchestra players can command, and will usually receive, premium fees. At present, such fees usually
range from $30 to $50 per lesson, but they can go
as high as $75 for a special coaching session with a
top performing artist. The average fee for lessons
from a highly qualified, experienced teacher is about
$20 or $25 per lesson. Teachers who are advanced
students themselves and are just beginning their
professional careers as performers and/or teachers
charge slightly less.

Young and eager teachers sometimes have more
to give their students than some professionals who
may be thinking more of their own performances
than the work of the students. Then too, some
older master teachers cannot communicate well with
beginners. But this is very much an individual matter. Most truly serious professional musicians consider it a special privilege to have the stimulation
of teaching younger players. They take the lessons
they give as seriously as they would a concert. There
are also teachers and coaches who themselves have
perhaps lacked that special emotional element a
performer must have and yet they have gone on to
become dedicated and excellent teachers. So, the
fact that your child's teacher may never have played
for a symphony orchestra or played a solo at one
of the great concert halls of the world does not

mean that he or she won't do a superb job with your child or won't command a top fee for lessons.

Just as rents, the cost of food and other staples of living vary greatly from one part of the country to another, so does the cost of music lessons. New York City rates are very high, and justifiably so. It is one of the world's important music centers and attracts some of the finest musicians and teachers. Other large cities which have outstanding performing groups and attract fine musicians will also have rates on the high side of the scale.

Contrary to what you might expect, it is usually cheaper to take lessons through a music school than it is to make arrangements with the *same* teacher privately. A teacher at a school almost always works for a lower fee than he charges private students. This is because it is often quite convenient for the teacher to work with a school. He doesn't have to worry about scheduling, collection of fees and cancellation of lessons and he doesn't have to rent a studio, use his own home or supply equipment. All he need do is arrive at the scheduled time and teach. Even though the school must make a profit on the transaction in order to stay in business, it almost always works out less expensively for the student. The difference for the same teacher for a single lesson may be as great as four or five dollars an hour.

The price per session depends on whether it is a group or private lesson. Group lessons are less expensive. But be wary of bargains. You will most often get what you pay for. Is your child's musical education a place to cut corners? Always be on guard against charlatans—they inhabit the music world, just as they do all other professions. Stay far away from teachers or schools of music advertising such miracles as learning how to play the piano beautifully in "ten easy lessons," or teachers who offer "money-back guarantees" or for that matter, guarantee any level of competence at any stage of instruction. Schools promoted with a barrage of advertising promising rich rewards to graduates or gifted students should also be avoided. There are no shortcuts and no guarantees in the study of music, whether it is popular piano, folk guitar or cello.

When do you pay for the lessons?

Most private teachers prefer to be paid by the month *in advance*. Work it out by multiplying the fee for one lesson times the number of lessons in any given month. When the teacher supplies the student with books or other equipment, payment should be made immediately or with the following month's tuition. Most people agree that this practice is more dignified and professional than the parent or student scrambling for the right change at the end of each lesson.

Many music schools set tuition by the school year and prefer to be paid in two or three installments in order to eliminate excessive bookkeeping. Be sure to check ahead of time on what financial arrangements are applicable should the student leave at mid-year. Some schools do not return the balance of the tuition unless *they* ask the student to leave. Others return a prorated portion of the fee. Inquire about possible tuition-refund insurance in case the student has a prolonged illness and cannot attend school.

Most schools will ask you to sign a form which is really a contract. Be sure you read and understand all the provisions, especially the manner of payment and the length of time for which you are signing up.

What about Makeup Lessons?

There are times when a scheduled lesson does not take place. If the teacher must cancel because of illness, a rehearsal, performance or other personal business, the situation is clear-cut. The teacher is obliged to make up the lesson at a mutually convenient time or to waive the fee for that lesson.

If the student cannot attend, he is almost always obligated to pay for the lesson—that is, the scheduled time—whether he is present or not. Such is the case at a music school: the teacher receives the full salary, regardless of how many students show up on any given day. Some private teachers, when given twenty-four or more hours' notice, may try to set up another lesson for the student during that week.

Find out about arrangements for holidays. A music school usually has a calendar showing what days the school will be closed. The yearly tuition is based on this schedule and it will not be altered. If you should decide to go on a vacation and take your music student along while school is in session, you will have to bear the loss.

Discuss your vacation plans with a private teacher far in advance; you may not be obligated to pay for missed lessons during a holiday period. These arrangements differ from teacher to teacher and it is most important not to take anything for granted. Discuss it well ahead of time and save trouble later.

What Should a Lesson Include?

The content of music lessons has changed a good deal in the past several decades. A student is now exposed to more than instrumental technique through rote learning. Music is studied (or should be) as a comprehensive subject with a much greater emphasis placed on *why*. Asking a child to practice scales without explaining why the scales are important and useful is taking that child for granted—it is unfair and bad practice. Instrumental lessons should generally include the following:

1. Rote scale and arpeggio material. (Chord material also for harmonic instruments such as piano.)
2. Some music theory, analysis and keyboard harmony. Ideally, all instrumentalists, not only pianists, should be exposed to some keyboard harmony in addition to the study of their own instrument. The keyboard provides an excellent visual and spatial medium for teaching and learning musical theory; all music students should be given some experience with it. As little as five minutes a week can be devoted to keyboard harmony with excellent results. The goal for non-pianists is comprehension, not performance at the keyboard.
3. The study of solo material so that even the beginning student may have an immediate *musical* experience. It is particularly important for the beginner to learn short solo pieces by ear and by rote long before he would be capable of playing such material from the written page. Remember, we speak before we learn to read. Our ears should be made to work first!
4. The study of études and other technique-building materials.
5. The study of ensemble material. For the be-

ginner, this is most often in the form of duets with the teacher but it should progress into the serious ensemble literature for the advanced instrumentalist.
6. Regular sight-reading work.
7. Transposition practice.
8. Regular memorizing of solo material.

How Can You Tell If the Teacher Is Doing a Good Job?

No teacher can do a good job with a child unless they can work together productively. If your child looks forward to his weekly lessons and comes home from each lesson with refreshed motivation and drive, you can be fairly certain there is a good relationship. If, on the other hand, there is continued apathy or resistance to practicing and lessons, then something is probably wrong.

You can tell a great deal about the kind of lesson your child is getting from what is written in his assignment notebook. (Most competent teachers will write out a student's assignment for the following week giving all appropriate information so the child can practice with a purpose and cover the assignment properly. A teacher may even specify the amount of time to be spent on each element if she feels the child needs such specific instruction.) If the lesson is comprehensive, and includes all or most of the elements mentioned above, home assignments will also contain most of the same elements: some theory, keyboard harmony, rote scale and arpeggio materials, études and other study material, solos, sight-reading and memorization. Obviously, all these elements won't show up every week, but they should be given on a regular basis.

Even if you are not much of a musician yourself,

you will be able to tell if your child is making progress. You know your child's learning capabilities quite well by the time he begins music lessons. His musical progress should parallel his other academic accomplishments as far as learning speed and comprehension are concerned.

Do not make an "agonizing reappraisal" after only two or three lessons. Let the relationship and the learning process get well underway before you look at it critically. Some students are slow starters and then make up for lost time when they are ready. It takes most teachers a while to get to know the capabilities of a student, how much to expect and how to draw it out of the student. Ask your child about his lessons and listen to what he says about the teacher and what takes place.

If you have any doubts or questions about lesson content, your child's progress, problems about practicing or any such things, do not hesitate to talk with the teacher. Such a conversation between parent and teacher is important, even when things seem to be going beautifully. A parent can often give valuable information about the student's attitudes or practice habits. The teacher can give the parent a perspective on his child that he has never had before. If this relationship is harmonious, it can greatly benefit the student.

When you have such a discussion with the teacher, either in person or over the telephone, be certain the child is not present. There is nothing potentially more destructive than having a supposedly private conversation about your child's capabilities, weaknesses and overall development only to discover that the child has overheard it. Often, the child should be consulted ahead of time and he should certainly be informed of some of the content of the discussion afterwards. It may be enlightening and encouraging for him to know about it. Although it is important to be honest with a child, there are certain discussions he should not be a party to. Talk things over with the teacher when you are in doubt or dissatisfied. Try to establish a pleasant spirit of cooperation. A teacher who feels attacked or challenged by a parent is not likely to be understanding and cooperative. Guard against calling the teacher too often. You will make a nuisance of yourself and this is likely to injure the relationship your child has with the teacher. Try to stay quietly in the background, ready with the right kind of support when necessary. If legitimate complaints lead you to urgent discussions with the music teacher more than two or three times during the school year, you had better think of changing teachers.

If, after a dozen or so lessons and after discussions with the teacher, you still feel the teacher is wrong for your child, because of a personality mismatch or unsatisfactory teaching, you should make a change. Try to do this in a way that will be the least upsetting to the child. If you reach a decision in the spring and the arrangement isn't really destructive, the most gentle way to make the break is to stop lessons at the summer vacation and begin with a new teacher in the fall. If you make the decision earlier in the year, then it would be a waste of your child's time to prolong the situation. Ideally, a new teacher should be chosen before halting lessons with the old one, so there is little or no gap in the routine of studying. Discuss the situation with your child and tell him why you think a change is desirable. It can be a simple, matter-of-fact statement such as: "You are older now and ready for a different kind of teacher." Or, "I know you have not been very happy with the way things have been going with your present teacher. I think I have found someone who will help make it more interesting and exciting for you."

Advanced students are often required to audition for a prospective teacher. The student should find out what kind of material the new teacher would like him to prepare for the audition. If such information is not available, then use the following as a guide. A new teacher will want to observe certain things about the student's level of development. Prepare something from the serious repertoire of the instrument in order to display overall musicianship and tone. Prepare some étude material that will display technical proficiency. The teacher may ask the student to do some sight-reading and to play some scales and arpeggios as well.

If the lessons are with a private teacher, do not feel embarrassed about telling him or her that you are going to make other arrangements. If your child is enrolled in a music school, discuss the problem with the director of the school and request another teacher who will better suit your child. In either case, be honest. Even in a large city like New York, musicians and music teachers are a fairly small and closed circle. They perform together, attend concerts together, socialize and discuss their students together. It is far better for a teacher to learn your intentions directly from you rather than inadvertently from the next teacher.

It is not as painful a confrontation as you might expect. Tell the teacher you have decided to make a change because, while you know he is capable, there seems to be a mismatch of personality or temperament. Or tell him you feel your child has become so comfortable and passive in the relationship that perhaps a change of teachers would be revitalizing.

For the experienced teacher, this is a routine matter. He may very well help you through the "ordeal" by agreeing with you, perhaps even recommending a teacher who he thinks might be better suited to your child's needs. You may even discover that you and the teacher (and your child) share a sense of relief that an awkward experience has ended.

Occasionally, a teacher will wish to give up a pupil. A conscientious teacher will not continue with a pupil if there seems to be a valid reason for making a change. Parents should guard against interpreting this situation as a failure for the child, or as a sign that the child is "unmusical" and should give up musical study completely.

There are several reasons a teacher might recommend a change. He may sense a personality clash. He may feel the student requires either a more formal or a more permissive teacher. He may feel strongly that the child is not well suited to the instrument he is studying and should try another. A parent should be grateful for this sort of advice. There is no need for a child to "hate music," simply because he is studying an instrument that does not suit him.

At a music school, the present teacher and director have probably discussed your child's needs before you have been asked to come in. They will usually suggest either a specific teacher change within the school or an instrument change.

People make mistakes. The best-informed and best-intentioned parents and teachers sometimes wind up in undesirable situations. Discuss it honestly with your child and explain that by making the change you hope his musical life will be happier and more satisfying.

Music Lessons as Physical or Emotional Therapy—the Handicapped Child

If your child is physically or emotionally handicapped, should you provide him with music lessons? The handicapped child needs music lessons, as well as all other expanding experiences, even more than the typical child. Doctors, therapists and educators have become increasingly aware of the emotional and physical advantages of music in the life of the handicapped child. This is a growing field of specialization for music educators.

There are two types of handicapped youngsters who can benefit greatly from a musical experience: one, those children with physical deficiencies ranging from poor motor control and coordination to paralysis of limbs; two, those children who suffer from emotional disorders or have minimal brain damage causing perceptual-learning problems.

For both the physically and emotionally handicapped child who has suffered through the experience of failure in many undertakings, the study of a musical instrument provides an excellent opportunity to accomplish and achieve success in something special and important. This can greatly aid the emotional well-being of the individual by increasing his self-respect, confidence and pride.

Free body movement and dance in response to music are excellent tension-releasing activities as well as a means of strengthening overall motor control and coordination. Just as a blind person learns to "see" with his ears and other senses, so the physically handicapped person learns to use the rest of his body to overcome his particular problem. I have watched a "Thalidomide baby" whose tiny fingers were formed at the elbow, learn to play a recorder in a group with "normal" ten-year-olds and do a superior job of it. Any child paralyzed from the waist down but whose arms and hands function normally can do very well on almost any instrument.

With a more severely handicapped person, we should try to provide a rewarding, successful outlet. The goals of instrumental study are somewhat different. But do not underestimate the will of a handicapped child who is determined. That will, plus your realistic encouragement and support, can produce remarkable results.

For the emotionally handicapped person, music can provide a vital experience in socialization and perhaps offer the setting for emotional expression and human contact which might not otherwise exist. The playing of a musical instrument, or singing and dancing can be a major emotional outlet and a satisfying group experience.

The child with minimal brain damage or a perceptual-learning disability may be able to achieve great success in the study of an instrument. His learning problems are usually specific and do not affect the overall process. And this child needs success and achievement more than most. In addition, the study of an instrument can provide an experience in organized, structured learning with rules and routines and patterns that will aid the development of his self-discipline.

These special children (or adults) need special teachers who, in addition to being excellent music teachers, also have training in the education of the physically and emotionally handicapped. The key to success in this vital area of education is the skill and sensitivity of the teacher. Some music schools have such special teachers and classes. Ask your child's doctor about the availability of such programs in your area. If he doesn't know of any, he may be able to tell you who to contact for information. Also contact the local school board, members of community action groups or write to your city or state education headquarters. Don't give up. Your child can obtain enormous benefits if you persist.

2

Practicing

"If you don't do your practicing instead of watching that television set all afternoon, I'm going to stop your music lessons. Your father works hard for his money and we're not going to throw it away on lessons if you won't even practice."

This dialogue is from a scene that has been played in millions of households. It is just as upsetting for the parent as it is for the child. Most parents, even while in the midst of such a scene, realize the negative effect of their words. Such a situation creates ill will and hostility between parent and child.

The art of practicing, indeed, the art of planning one's time in general, must be learned. The same applies to homework. No parent would be likely to say: "If you don't do your homework, I won't let you go to school any more." Practicing must be taught; it can be learned. The parent's role, to help reinforce and encourage, is very important. The rest of this chapter will offer some guidelines.

What is good practicing?

The first important prerequisite is that the student know exactly what is expected of him. He must be aware of his immediate goals and be prepared to work toward what he must accomplish for the next lesson. This means that the teacher is obligated to define the goals and provide the student with the proper means of "attacking" the lesson on his own. In order for the child to know this, the assignment should almost always be *written out in detail*, in the order in which the work should be tackled at each practice session. This will help the student structure his own practice time and monitor his own progress. Armed with a well-structured and written-out assignment, a student can march through the week's preparations toward a specific goal.

Encourage your child to follow the written assignment when he is practicing. But try not to discourage his interludes of improvising and experimenting. It may sound to you like a musical form of doodling—and in a way that is just what it is—but it can be a vital part of the child's creative development and exploration of sound. You can, for example, comment favorably on the interesting "effects" he has discovered.

Naturally, this doodling cannot replace any of the regular practice material, but it is a desirable supplement. If it seems to consume more time than the assigned work, you might suggest that he finish the regular practicing first and then do his improvising.

If he seems to have a genuine "creative flair," it would be wise to see if it has been noticed at lessons and discuss with the teacher ways of encouraging it. Perhaps a certain amount of improvising could be included in the lesson assignment in whatever way might be appropriate.

Some students can master a particular task in five minutes; others, equally bright, may need an hour for the same material. Why is this? Often it is simply a matter of concentration and the particular sense of understanding that a given student has for a

given assignment. Development of the skill of con-
centrating is one of the objectives of the first year
or two of learning in music. Both the teacher and
the parent should help the student begin to acquire
this skill.

What Is the Parents' Role?

The parents' attitude toward music education in
general is of primary importance in developing the
child's attitude toward his music lessons and his
practicing. It is not encouraging for a child to know
that his parents can't stand listening to his "noise"
when he practices. Students frequently are forced
to confide in their teachers the fact that they are
not allowed to practice after Daddy comes home
because "Daddy wants to relax and have it quiet."
Some parents may think it is amusing to report to
guests, "We make Johnny lock himself in the bath-
room when he practices his trumpet. Even then it
just about breaks our eardrums!" They may feel
they are saying this good-humoredly, but all too
often the message Johnny really gets is "My parents are just putting up with my trumpet lessons.
It is not a serious matter to them."

Whether the parent discusses his attitude with
the child or not isn't what matters. If parents believe that music lessons are a basic part of their
child's overall education; if parents feel that music
lessons do not depend upon temporary fluctua-
tions of interest or motivation any more than
studying arithmetic does, then the youngster will
react positively in almost every case. If, however,
parents think music lessons are only for the child
who is self-motivated, self-disciplined, well organized and "talented," then the child will soon get
the message and react accordingly. What child—

indeed, what adult—possesses all the most desirable traits in such abundance that he does not need reassurance, steady encouragement and imposed discipline from time to time?

A positive parental attitude is crucial. You are not "trying music lessons for a while," once you start. They will be as much an ongoing study as the rest of the child's schooling. A parent needs all the skill he can muster. How much to interfere and direct? How much to allow "nature to take its course?" Most children at about nine or ten can learn to practice independently. The less a child shows such ability, the more a teacher and parent must see to it that each lesson and the proper practice routine are carefully written down. But, it is an error to consider a child's ability to practice by himself as a test of his interest in music. Many children are dependent for a long time on the active cooperation and approval of the older members of the household.

Those parents (and we might include older brothers and sisters here) who themselves have an active interest in music and can actually give specific help during practice are encouraged to do so. Enthusiasm and warmth and that special sense of rapport with the practicer mean even more than the ability to help with specific technical problems.

How long should a child practice each day?

There are several factors which enter into this: the child's age and level of maturity, including his attention span; his level of advancement on the instrument; the fatigue factors of the specific instrument that is being studied.

The teacher recommends the approximate practice time per day for each student. It is usually between a half hour and one full hour. For very young students and beginners, less than a half hour may be satisfactory. Very advanced students who are planning to pursue a serious career in music may have to put in much more than an hour each day.

But the most important factor is *regularity*. Far more than the duration of each practice period, the sitting down each and every day establishes the habits of playing that are vital. Fifteen minutes of concentrated practicing each day will do more for a student than two hours one day and nothing more for the rest of the week. There is nothing wrong with missing one day occasionally, but a student should not take a "vacation" every weekend.

Don't encourage practice sessions which are so long they become drudgery for your child. It is sometimes better to divide the total recommended time into two shorter sessions each day. A half hour per day can be divided easily into two fifteen-minute sessions, separated by completely unrelated activities—eating, playing, reading—so the child will approach each of the short sessions with a freshness and alertness that will greatly improve the quality of his work.

*Provide a regularly scheduled practice
period each day.*

Schedule his daily practice session or sessions at very specific times that fit in smoothly with his daily routine. Work this out with your child. If he helps to set the routine, he will be much more apt to follow it. It is his responsibility and he must have a say in working it out.

Some children get up very early in the morning and can put in an excellent session after breakfast, before going to school. Of course this is only possible if it doesn't interfere with sleeping neighbors or other family members! Right after dinner or an afternoon snack are also possible times. The specific schedule differs greatly from family to family. But once it is established, it should be followed as closely as possible. This avoids a daily hassle and confrontation. It gives the child the framework within which to work and teaches him to organize his time in a productive manner.

There is plenty of time in a day for a well-organized young person to play with his friends, watch television, eat, do his school work, practice and even take a bath! If your child has trouble fitting all this into his day, then you can be sure that one of the above items is consuming too much time, or else you have overcommitted his time. It is self-evident that you cannot schedule a child (or allow him to schedule himself) for Boy Scouts one afternoon, fencing lessons the next, religious instruction the next, music lessons the next and so on throughout the week, and expect him to accomplish anything more than turning himself into a nervous wreck. A child should have some free, unscheduled time to himself.

Most parents are anxious to give their children the best of everything. Instead, many children are so overfed on activities that they develop a sort of intellectual indigestion. They rebel against the routine and everything in it. Often, music is lost as a result, and not because the child dislikes music.

Here are a few other suggestions that may help you avoid confrontations and encourage positive attitudes.

1. Avoid scheduling the practice period before a meal or a snack. People do not work well on an empty stomach. It is very distracting!

2. Try not to schedule a practice session when

other cherished activities are taking place—even if they seem unimportant to you. It will only foster a resentment of practicing and teach the child to hate music.

3. Be impersonal when reminding a child that it is practice time. Avoid emotion and nagging. Tell him simply: "It is five o'clock." Or, "Would you like a snack before practicing?"

4. One of the best ways for a child to develop responsibility is for the parents to give up the controls. If a child knows that you are *always* there to remind him to do his work, it means he never has to bother to remind himself.

One child who was accustomed to such a parental crutch came home from school one day and announced to his mother that he had a science report due in one week. He was used to daily reminders and nagging from his mother and so gave *her* the assignment schedule and thus relieved himself of the responsibility. This time the mother decided she had had enough. She told the child it was his assignment and it was up to him to see that it was done. The week went by and nothing was said. The child did nothing. On the morning the report was due the mother casually asked: "Is the report ready to hand in?" The child was furious. "It is your fault. You didn't remind me to do it!"

One way to encourage children to take over the controls is to let them know that the parent will not be the "policeman." A child can learn a great deal from not practicing one week and going unprepared to a lesson. It is painful, but it can be very effective, provided the parent isn't negative. It is hard, but try to avoid saying: "See, it's your own fault for not practicing." The child is only too aware of this new "fact of life." Something like this can be more helpful: "It must have really upset you to have to sit through an unprepared lesson." Some understanding of the predicament at this point will do a great deal to reestablish the child's confidence and to show that nothing disastrous has taken place. A parent who can be sympathetic at a time like that is a parent who can be trusted!

Provide a place for practice which is not violated by others.

It is very important that both sound and sight distractions be removed as much as possible. You should try to come as close as you can to ideal working conditions. Distractions can be minimized if a child has his own room where he can close the door, or he can use some other closed-off area in the house or apartment. If the piano is in the living room or dining room, then it is important that other family members cooperate and keep out of the way.

Provide adequate light.

This seems almost too obvious to mention but it is often neglected. To work with poor lighting is not only bad for one's eyes but it also increases fatigue, cuts down on work efficiency and undermines concentration.

See that the child's instrument is stored in a convenient place.

One of the advantages of the piano is that it doesn't have to be set up each time one wants to play it. Virtually every other instrument must be set up, after the case is taken from its accustomed place.

Make that place as convenient as possible. Otherwise, it is another barrier to "getting started."

Provide a handy place for music and supplies.

If all the necessary items are stored at the practice location, the student need not wander through the house gathering his materials. We all know things have a way of getting lost once they are scattered in different places. It is a very common problem with young students. Either the assignment book is missing, or the solo book—or something! Once again, getting started is dependent on being able to have everything handy and in its proper place.

Provide a music stand.

Unless the child is a pianist (and every piano comes with its own built-in stand), you should provide a proper music stand. It can be purchased very reasonably (an inexpensive portable one for about $10, a sturdy professional model for $25 or $30) and will encourage the child to sit up correctly with proper posture. It also will eliminate the problem of falling music, fumbling with the instrument and the like. In short, everyone will feel more comfortable and "professional."

Provide a metronome only if the teacher requests it.

A metronome is a device that ticks off a steady beat at whatever speed one sets it. It can be a valuable teaching aid in specific circumstances. It can also be detrimental to the child's musical growth when incorrectly or excessively used.

A metronome is not meant for a beginner. A young

music student must learn to establish and maintain a steady pulse at different speeds. Different teachers use different methods to instruct a pupil in this skill. But it is generally accepted today that this skill must develop from within a child and not from an imposed device like the metronome, which only serves to confuse the young student and make him preoccupied with this outside stimulus. We learn to walk without crutches; so the student must concentrate his efforts on establishing the steady pulse himself.

The metronome does have two very specific functions for the more advanced musician. It can be used to exert discipline in technical studies and to maintain the steady pulse when the complex rhythmic subdivisions of the beat in an exercise or composition are being worked out.

Handling the inevitable recessions.

They are a normal part of the learning process and we all know what these study recessions are. Indeed much of a child's social and physical development follows a familiar pattern. A plateau is reached; it doesn't look as if anything has been happening for a long time. Then all of a sudden the child wakes up one morning and has learned to walk!

Infrequent and relatively short recessions are expected by any understanding parent and any experienced teacher. These periods affect all learners, however bright or zealous. A call to the teacher to make her aware that a recession is in progress at home is often a great help. It needn't be a distress call, but simply one to provide information. If the teacher is aware of what is happening, she can often rekindle a pupil's normal enthusiasm by providing a new and exciting piece of music to work on. Or a new technique or skill can be started. Or the teacher may spend a whole lesson playing for (and hopefully inspiring) the recessionist student! Sometimes taking a student to an exciting concert at such a time can provide the necessary boost.

These short-range recessions can sometimes be caused by a new stimulation in the child's life—a new sport, a new friend or whatever. Occasionally, it is a new anxiety, an illness or death in the family, the arrival of a new baby. But most often recessions can be traced to one of two causes. The first is the basic impediment to most learning: a natural resistance to moving from a just mastered step to an unfamiliar new one. The second root cause of most recessions is overall tiredness and the difficulty of getting back in gear after an interruption (illness or vacation) of two weeks or more.

The parent's role in a recession is to provide as much encouragement and understanding as possible. Scolding and threats are not helpful. It is natural for a parent to feel anxious and irritable if he sees that the child is suffering from recessionitis. But the child should avoid having to feel guilty or anxious about the recession. Recognize the recession, but don't make it more important than it is by "confronting" the child with its evidence. It will help if you tell him that these recessions are a normal part of growth and learning and that they happen to everyone at some time or other.

One of the most common times of the year for both student and teacher recessions is February. The winter can be long and dreary—the Christmas vacation has long since come and gone; the Easter holiday is still a good way off. Some teachers regularly anticipate this and schedule a March recital which can add the incentive and spark to keep their students going during that stretch of the year.

If the recession lasts longer than a month or two,

or if it recurs frequently, then the parent must take it as a significant warning signal that something may be wrong. The best way to find out about the problem is to discuss it with the child. Often parents consider asking the child as something akin to the last resort. But that should be the starting place. Perhaps it is the wrong instrument, the wrong teacher or something else that can only come out through casual conversation with the child. It is hoped that the child will feel free enough to express his feelings and thoughts. If he knows that you care enough, he is bound to communicate these thoughts with you.

I remember a young girl of nine who wanted desperately to study the violin. Her parents arranged for private lessons for her at a music school and she did remarkably well. She was truly a "natural" on the instrument. She was highly endowed with musical sensitivity, and self-motivated and well-disciplined in the bargain—an ideal setup for success.

Then, with no warning at all, she announced one day that she did not like the violin and wanted to stop lessons immediately. This was no recession, it was a full-fledged "crash." The teacher was shocked. The parents were shocked. What had happened? There was not a single clue. The child said she wished to switch from violin to piano. That was that.

Weeks later, quite by accident, it came out that a friend of this talented nine-year-old, who was about the same age and who had been studying violin for a longer time, had played with her. The friend was also talented and naturally more advanced through more study. This so "crushed" the young girl, despite the fact that she was a most promising beginner, that she vowed never to play the violin again!

An extreme case, you may say. Well, perhaps it is not typical, but it does illustrate the ways in which each child's situation may be affected. Both parent and teacher must be alert to the factors which may cause either a mild or serious recession. Often the cause can be quickly diagnosed and a remedy found. Be ready for these downturns; allow the child to have them honorably and to find an honorable way of working out of them. A recession overcome often finds a more-confident-than-ever student surging foward with a new sense of excitement and discovery, and a smiling parent and teacher observing, quite properly, from the wings.

What about the summer vacation?

When it comes to decisions about summer plans for your child's musical life, take your cues from him. Everyone, young and old, needs a vacation from routines and schedules. The summer can be a time for choice and freedom. Let me state right away my belief that there is absolutely no harm in a child taking a full summer vacation from music, if he so chooses. The average student needs only a few weeks in September to get back into shape and to be approximately at the point where he or she left off the preceding June.

Some children wish to continue with their private lessons over the summer. In that case, it is usually a fine thing to do as the child will be able to progress without the usual pressures of school work. And he may thrive on the stimulation of a scheduled activity. If he does take summer lessons, try to schedule the daily practice session for the morning before the day becomes too hot and while the child is fresh and alert. This will also help eliminate interference with various summer activities your child will want to participate in during the rest of the day.

Let the child decide. If he chooses not to take lessons, then that is probably best for him. Perhaps he had a difficult winter, with many social, intellectual or emotional stresses. Although forced lessons over the summer can only be counterproductive, some informal community musical activity might be an excellent choice. Many schools have developed summer bands and orchestras which meet daily or several times a week and even give regular concerts. This is often great fun and will help keep the music student "in shape" while he is not formally practicing. It can also provide a new incentive that may carry over into the fall.

For the student who does not wish summer lessons, a teacher will often provide a new solo book or duet book that he can play from with a friend (or family member). This material can be given just before the beginning of summer vacation to encourage a bit of musical activity, if not a more formal schedule.

The highly motivated "serious" music student may ask to go to a music or arts camp over the summer. Choose such a camp carefully. Some parents are so delighted when their children seem as eager to "achieve" that they inadvertently place them in an unhealthy atmosphere of intense competition which does exist in some specialized camps and schools. This can be self-defeating. A previously eager music student can return from a summer spent with a group so talented and anxious to compete that all his eagerness is drained and a feeling of hopelessness has replaced his confidence.

However, there are many good music camps where care is taken to avoid this sort of thing. It can be an excellent experience for a child who wants (and can take) a summer of intensive music work along with regular camp life. Such a camp ordinarily provides fine ensemble opportunities and performing experiences with other students of similar abilities. It can be as good for one child as it may be disastrous for another. Let your child's feelings be the guiding factor.

A few words for professionals.

If you are a professional musician (or a very advanced amateur) or a music teacher yourself, you are in a unique position as a parent. It is, of course, true that you can help your child with technical practicing problems more than the average parent. And you are in a better position to evaluate the capabilities of your child's music teacher or the quality of the school music curriculum. You can do much to foster and help your child's progress. But you are also in a unique position to prevent progress!

Because of your knowledge and your emotional involvement with your child, you may demand too much, too soon. You may, without intending to, set far too high a standard of achievement. This sort of unrealistic goal can cause the child to turn away from music.

Just because a music student is the child of a professional musician does not mean he will necessarily be outstanding. His attitude toward lessons is likely to depend to a great extent on the relationship he has with you. If music has always been an area of great enjoyment in your home, he will probably be eager to join in. But if it is an area of tension and pressure, if your anxiety shows through, he may very well shy away from it.

Help him with practicing if and when he asks for your help. Otherwise, leave him alone. Avoid becoming a second teacher at home. Your presence can only be an asset to your child if you have a healthy relationship in the first place. If your child enjoys working with you, then your help and participation can be beneficial. If you can remain relatively unemotional and patient and can provide generous helpings of praise and encouragement, then both you and your child are fortunate indeed.

You know yourself best. If you tend to become critical and impatient, you can probably do the most good by staying clear of the practice area unless your presence is specifically requested by your child. You know too whether your child enjoys listening to your concerts or practice sessions, whether there is an easy "give-and-take" or whether the storm clouds gather rapidly when the two generations are making music together.

It is a great joy when members of a family can come together to make music harmoniously. But if the personalities tend toward dissonance in that situation, then it should be avoided until parent and child can develop the maturity and find the technique to play or practice together.

3

Singing

How often have you heard an adult say that he is "tone deaf," that he is just a "monotone" and can't sing a note, that he always was and always will be a "listener?"

The ability to carry a tune is as remarkable and complex a human phenomenon as the ability to speak. But both of these skills develop naturally in the vast majority of young children as part of their informal early childhood learning. It is done by simple observation and imitation.

Almost every adult who considers himself a listener has been talked into that state early in life by an inconsiderate and ill-informed parent or teacher. Inhibitions are easy to acquire and very difficult to remove. Good habits and attitudes are every bit as easy to learn as bad ones. You, the parent and the teacher, can make all the difference.

There is great variety in children's voice development, just as in their rates of physical, emotional and intellectual growth. The development of overall vocal-auditory responses in any one child is a very individual business. Just as some children learn to walk and to talk faster or slower than others and some people get their teeth earlier or later than the so-called norm, the ability to carry a tune develops at different speeds and at different ages.

It is unfortunate that there are very few scientific

studies in this field. The principle that seems to have held up through years of observation by many in the field of music education is that there is a close correlation between age of learning and the amount of early exposure, in the home or in a group setting, to informal, uninhibited singing in an atmosphere of pleasure and enjoyment.

If a child observes those around him singing and enjoying it as a part of everyday living, he seems to imitate this behavior readily, just as he imitates the speech he hears. The quality of the singing does not seem to be particularly important. A parent or teacher who does not sing in tune or with a pleasing tone-quality can stimulate a child's singing response just as well as someone who is blessed with more skill or a more naturally beautiful tone. The key factor seems to be the degree of enthusiasm, naturalness and pleasure that the adult takes in the act of singing.

There is a very small group of children who are found to have some sort of hearing impairment or other physical disability which may prevent a relatively normal development of the ability to sing in tune. If your child falls into this category, then you have a special obligation to help him overcome the problem and to give him every opportunity to find and develop his voice to its fullest extent.

A small percentage of any average group of children are simply "late bloomers" in their ability to carry a tune. Parents of such children are also obligated to see to it that such children do not fall prey to circumstances that will inhibit or thwart the natural growth process. If there is no physical disability involved, the child will learn naturally to carry a tune provided he is not detoured en route by an ego-damaging experience. Some children are not even aware they are not singing in tune and will join in group singing with much vigor and enthusiasm. Here it is the job of the skillful music teacher to prevent group teasing or ridicule. Children will readily accept the simple statement of fact that some people learn to sing in tune faster and earlier than others. In a group situation, children can often be helpful and encouraging to one another if the parent or teacher creates the right atmosphere. A weak singer need never be singled out and embarrassed in front of the group. It is not helpful to be told to listen instead of sing because "you are spoiling the sound of the group." Rather, he should be surrounded by strong singers and his difficulties simply ignored in the group. Auditions for the Metropolitan Opera are still a long way off. Who knows? By then, the late bloomer may be ahead of the rest!

There are a number of helpful exercises which can be employed. These involve matching tones and singing high and then low, beginning with the wide jump of an octave and eventually narrowing it down to the smaller intervals. These exercises can be part of a chorus warm-up—all singers benefit from them—to help children who have specific problems develop their vocal-auditory responses without being embarrassed. These youngsters need encouragement and should be told that there is nothing very special about their situation. Some people get their molars earlier or later than others—so it is with the voice. And if a continuing group singing experience is provided for these children, they will almost surely develop their natural abilities. They must be made to believe it is just a matter of time and experience before they will sing in tune.

If a young child has had the misfortune to be labeled a monotone or a listener, he is likely to act accordingly unless steps are taken to overcome such early training. Children tend to fill the role that is set for them by adults.

Adolescence and the changing voice.

Adolescence does not begin or end suddenly, nor does it occur at a set point. It is a period of emotional stress for some young people, not only because of glandular changes within the body, but because of environmental conditions based on changing social relationships.

When a boy's voice changes, his vocal chords begin to lengthen as his body reaches a rapid growth period. During this time a boy often has very little control over his voice in terms of pitch. With some, this change (going down approximately one octave) comes rapidly; with others, it may take from one to three years. A girl's voice also changes in range and quality. Girls do not generally experience any difficulty managing their voices during this period and the changes are not nearly as pronounced as they are for boys.

The individual pace of development in this period causes an enormous range of variation within any adolescent group. While the adolescent badly needs the acceptance of his peers, at the same time he is quite sensitive to his awkwardness and will often react strongly against giggling, teasing or being singled out. It is important then, to try to establish an accepting emotional and social framework at school and at home. This will help to ameliorate the dread which many adolescents have of using their voices during this period.

If a child arrives at this point in life having had a happy experience with music and singing, it is relatively easy to help him adjust to this new but

temporary awkwardness. If he has had the misfortune to be labeled a listener or monotone, the additional stresses of adolescence will not make this
a prime time to change his self-image as a singer.
The moral of the tale is simple. Do everything
possible to help the late bloomer receive the necessary help and practice before adolescence, so that
he may have the advantage of entering this period
with a secure and healthy attitude about himself
and singing for pleasure.

One useful approach is to present the adolescent
group with the physiological facts about voice
changes in a serious and scientific manner. This can
do much to relieve tension and avoid the teasing
that sometimes takes place. Understanding is often
a relief. Parents and teachers would do well to take
a casual attitude and avoid making the problem
seem larger than it is.

There is more than one theory about adolescent
voices, but everyone seems to agree that pupils
should continue to sing throughout the period of
voice change. A boy needs much encouragement
from the teacher and should not be made to feel
that changing voices are not pleasing in quality.
The range may be quite limited for a short period
of time and it may be difficult to maintain a steady
pitch, since there is an uncertainty about just how
to produce a clear tone with a changing voice.
Teachers and parents can help most by showing
encouragement and confidence in a boy's ability to
learn to control his changing voice as well as his
changing body.

One more word to quell any anxieties that may
arise at this time: there is no reason at all to believe
that singing during the period of voice change will
in any way cause either temporary or permanent
damage to the vocal apparatus. Repeated loud

singing with the voice used improperly will of course cause discomfort. But no real damage is caused by young voices loudly singing the school fight song or the latest rock sensation.

Sight-singing.

In the introduction to this book we discussed the fact that music is a language. Since voice is man's basic musical instrument, ideally he should learn to sing by ear and then from musical notation—just as we learn to reproduce the sounds of the language by ear or by rote before we learn to read it.

A prominent Metropolitan Opera star was once overheard remarking: "I'm not a musician. I'm a singer!" Unfortunately this was not meant as a joke. It is too often the case with vocal students and professional singers alike.

All music students should learn to use voice as one of their musical instruments. All voice students should study the language of music and become familiar with its aural and its written vocabulary. The singer should be a musician first and a singer second.

Learning to sing from written notation is a very important basic skill for all music students. There is an enormous range of abilities: from the simplest level, being able to recognize the direction of a melody or the difference between a step and a jump in a melody, a student can progress to the point where he can sight-sing atonal music using the difficult fixed-do system. Although the vocal student has to develop his sight-singing ability to the most advanced levels, all music students should learn basic sight-singing skills as part of their comprehensive music education.

Most music educators today realize that rote repetition has been overused in the teaching of singing, just as the written page has been overused in the teaching of instrumental playing. Instrumentalists need to learn to use their ears more and be able to play freely, without being slaves to musical notation. Jazz musicians, of course, do develop their improvisational skills to the fullest. Singers need to develop more skill at singing from notation without relying so heavily on hearing and then imitating. It is quite remarkable to see the number of fine professional and amateur singers who seem a bit lost and insecure when required to do some sight-reading.

Sight-singing actually involves a number of separate skills. When song material is used, the text is often dropped temporarily so the student can focus his full attention on the musical notation. Sight-singing is more than merely reading the pitches and reproducing them. It includes correct phrasing, rhythm, dynamics and articulation. Ultimately a good deal of attention must also be paid to the pronunciation and meaning of the text to be sung.

One of the basic sight-singing methods you may hear a good deal about is called solfeggio, in which the degrees of the scale are identified by the "sol-fa" syllables.

The most difficult application of this system but probably the best for training the really serious music student is the *fixed-do method*. When this is used, the natural scale is sung with the syllables do, re, mi, fa, sol, la, ti. This has been quite successful, perhaps because of the rigorous training and practice of the students who are exposed to it. It is certainly the best form of sight-singing when applied to modern atonal music, because it does not orient around a fixed tonal center. Most music composed today has no harmonic tonality to which the singer can cling for support.

Another application of solfeggio is the *movable-do system*. With this, the syllable *do* always represents the tonic or the tonal center, regardless of the key in which the piece is written. It is this tonal orientation that makes the movable-do system somewhat easier than the fixed-do method. When the piece modulates to a new key, the new tonic is called do. This system emphasizes the relationship between the degrees of the scale and helps the user develop a feeling for tonality.

Another method uses numbers instead of syllables. The scale is represented by 1, 2, 3, 4, 5, 6, 7, 8 (or high 1). This system works in somewhat the same manner as the movable-do. It is a good method to use with young children or less-experienced students because the numbers are more readily identified with the various degrees of the scale. Since musical training begins with tonal music, the beginner can do quite well with either the movable-do or the number system. When he is ready for atonal sight-singing he can then substitute a single syllable, such as La, for singing on all pitches. This is a good bit easier for most students than applying the fixed-do and is quite adequate for all but the most serious and dedicated music students.

It should be noted that most music teachers swear by the specific sight-singing method they are accustomed to using. It is hard to blame them, for one becomes quite comfortable with a system after a while. Advocates of the fixed-do method in particular feel that it is the only proper method and that it is really no more difficult for a young student than any other method. It has the true advantage of being workable with any and all sorts of music, tonal or atonal. It also provides more musical syllables on which to sing than the number system.

The Hungarian composer, Zoltán Kodály, invented a hand signal to represent each of the solfeggio syllables of the scale (see page 146). This is an interesting visual aid that can be used most successfully with singing from notation. It is also a valid method of rote teaching, and a form of sign language, similar to that used by the deaf.

Perfect and relative pitch.

Pitch memory is a fascinating phenomenon. "Perfect pitch," as it is called, is the ability to "recall" and reproduce the exact pitch of a given note. It is not known if people are born with this ability or if it develops at an early age. Perhaps both are possible. Somewhere between five and ten percent of the population seems to have perfect pitch, although there are no really accurate studies of the distribution. Perhaps the percentage is in fact higher, but many people simply don't realize they possess this unusual ability.

There doesn't seem to be any question that an acute sense of "relative pitch" can be developed with practice and training. Relative pitch is the ability to reproduce the exact pitch once you are oriented to the scale by being given any one pitch.

Some music educators believe that learning to sing with the fixed-do method helps to develop a sense of perfect pitch. The do is always the same sound and after a while it begins to implant itself in a musician's mind.

Perfect pitch can be a great asset when sight-singing. It can also become a hardship of sorts when singing or playing in a group which does not stay perfectly in tune, or when reading music that is being spontaneously transposed. The owner of a perfect-pitch ear finds it hard to accept something that is "wrong." Most of us just accept the new tone as C and proceed accordingly. The person with perfect pitch doesn't find it easy to sing or play a D or B when the note reads C.

For a conductor, an ear which is very finely trained and acutely sensitive to pitch is a great asset. Sometimes the members of the group he is conducting, however, find it hard to live with a conductor whose sense of pitch is so "perfect."

The main thing is that the ear can be trained to hear better and can become more sensitive to pitch. Constant practice provides an auditory conditioning that leads to increased accuracy. A conscious effort by a student to improve through deliberate listening can often bring a young musician to the point where he can be virtually certain that he has almost perfect pitch. It is like the development of a good sense of observation. If you open your eyes and try to be more aware of what you see, you will find your eyes taking in more and more. It isn't that your eyesight is improving, but rather that your brain is using more of the impulses being sent to it by your eyes. So it is with your ears, if you will only train yourself to listen with your brain.

Majoring in voice.

A good musical ear is the most important asset for anyone contemplating voice as a major instrument. There are other important requirements, but the ear is paramount for the singer, because he must rely almost totally upon it in order to produce the correct series of pitches.

Singing is a unique form of music-making because the singer uses words in addition to the other elements of music. A singer must be able to communicate a special sense of drama, of story, of content, which goes beyond the arrangement of sound.

This ability is an almost absolute requirement for anyone who wishes to take up any style of vocal delivery. From Lieder singer to blues chanter, the words must have meaning, and must be endowed with a special individual sense of interpretation. This is the extra challenge for the vocalist and if successfully met, it can provide great rewards.

Much of the singer's ability is totally natural—because of a favorable set of bones, sinus cavities, vocal cords and chest and throat structures. Most young students who wish to become voice majors have noticed or have been told by others that they have a better than average strength and quality of tone when they sing. For them, the sound flows out deeper, clearer, higher or lower, with more resonance and with greater ease than it does for others. Without some outstanding natural equipment, the singer has certain limitations that are nearly impossible to overcome.

The young child who seems to have an unusual vocal ability should be encouraged to make a strong start on some instrument other than voice. The piano is certainly the best choice if the student has the aptitude for it. The singer who can accompany himself and who has a thorough grounding in the language of music, as learned through the study of the piano, will make more rapid progress.

Most voice teachers agree that the best age to begin voice lessons is after puberty when the vocal chords have settled into their new range. It is important to choose a voice teacher very carefully. Because teaching singing seems to be a less exact art than teaching a musical instrument, there are a number of unqualified teachers in this area. A recommendation from a school music teacher or from a friend who has had first-hand experience with a particular teacher is often helpful. Also, one is relatively safe in finding a teacher through an accredited music school whose staff has certain basic teaching credentials as well as professional performing experience.

The psychological factors of tension, relaxation and mood are particularly significant with the voice student. Hence the chemistry between voice teacher and student must be excellent if proper progress is to take place.

A good voice teacher always gives instruction in the basic anatomy of the vocal chords and diaphragm so the student has an understanding of the concepts behind correct breathing techniques. Lessons usually include breathing exercises as proper breathing is the foundation for proper voice production. The vocal chords and the entire body must always be relaxed in order for the voice to develop properly without being damaged. The parent should always be on the lookout for the tense, strained sound of a forced voice. This is a sure sign that instruction is amiss. The emphasis should always be on producing a free, relaxed tone.

A motto often expressed by voice coaches is "Parla forte—Canta piano," which translates "Speak loudly—Sing softly." A skilled voice teacher will follow the range of the natural voice and through relaxation, will slowly extend the range at either end. Flexibility and lightness are key elements. There will also be a concentration on voice placement or focus of tone. Then too, lessons will include phrasing, musicianship concepts, and the techniques of the art of communication and enunciation. Many voice teachers ask their beginning students to use Italian, as it is a far easier language to sing than English. French and German are also preferable to English because they contain more open vowel sounds.

Singing provides great flexibility for anyone who majors in it: a variety of performance opportunities, both religious and secular, public and private; music from every period by virtually every composer for almost every imaginable combination of voices and instruments. The pleasures of singing combine with the fact that voice is the most portable and the most totally acceptable instrument we know. Those who choose to be really serious voice students have a particularly difficult climb. Not only is the greatest amount of technical study necessary, but a combination of fine musical sensitivity and excellent health is necessary to see them through. Singers, perhaps more than any other musicians, are subject to good days and bad days. The human voice will often betray the owner, even if he has only a relatively mild illness. A cold that would not bother a violinist can knock a singer out of action for a week. Tiredness, nervous strain, many of the concomitants of modern living, can wreak havoc with a singer's ability to "play well." So the physical, psychological and emotional factors have a special significance in the life of a singer. If a violin or clarinet goes out of order, it can be rushed to the repair shop and the concert can go on that night. Most professional instrumentalists own more than one instrument, so there is always one in perfect playing condition. With the human voice, this convenience is not possible.

4

Choosing an Instrument

Many parents—and their children—wonder which instrument they should learn to play. The real question is: "What instrument can I learn to play?" This chapter will help you answer that question.

The choice of instrument should not be haphazard, based on whatever instrument is handiest or cheapest or even most appealing or "socially acceptable." Because your neighbor has a clarinet which she will be glad to donate is no reason for your child to study the clarinet. Because you happen to own a piano or think one would look lovely in your living room is no reason to direct your child toward playing the piano. Because you play the flute beautifully is no reason to insist that your daughter do the same. And because the local school music teacher is desperate for a tuba player for the orchestra is no reason why your son should play the tuba.

Too often a child is called unmusical because he doesn't succeed on what was simply the "wrong" instrument for him. Too often a child with considerable musical sensitivity or talent grows up hating music because he was forced to study an instrument for which he was not suited temperamentally, physically or intellectually.

Helping your child make the proper choice of an instrument that is *most likely* to fit his individual assets and skills is one of the most important roles a parent can play in fostering the musical education of his child. There is, of course, no magic formula to assure a perfect choice, but the considerable information that is now available can make the decision sound and logical. Even a parent who is not familiar with instruments and musical language can do a great deal to reduce the "margin for error" when giving his children the opportunity to select an instrument.

There is a wide variation in what particular instruments demand of the player. It is rare to find a student who cannot handle some instrument well enough to benefit from studying it. A student should study an instrument for which he is well suited both physically and temperamentally. In other words, the chemistry between student and instrument should be right. The student should like the instrument and the kind of sound it makes. Occasionally one finds a youngster who has such a great desire to learn one instrument that this desire can compensate for a certain lack of natural aptitude. But there isn't any other reason why a child should start on an instrument for which only limited aptitude is shown.

It is also important to realize that a child shouldn't be obligated to continue the study of an instrument once it is apparent that the choice was not a good one. If you are lucky, finding the "right" instrument can happen quickly. But it may take considerable experimenting on various instruments. This is not a waste of time and money; rather, it can save needless pain, emotional upset and money later in the game.

Some young people seem to have been watched over carefully by the muse of music, for they are capable of handling virtually any instrument quite easily. For such a student personal preference is perhaps the only criterion. For most young people though, the choice is narrowed down at the start by the following natural conditions:

> *anatomical aptitude*
> *motor skill aptitude*
> *vocal-auditory aptitude*
> *intellectual and emotional aptitude, which includes*
> *the capacity to concentrate, to persist and to learn*
> *and retain skills systematically*

Each of these criteria will be discussed as we talk about the major families of instruments and their various members. Remember, there are lots of instruments to choose from. A little knowledge now, which you can use as a skillful parent, may help you guide your child to rewards and satisfactions which cannot be measured.

All musical instruments can be classified in three basic groups: String Instruments, Wind Instruments and Percussion Instruments.

String Instruments

The sound on all string instruments is produced by the vibrating of stretched strings. The three methods by which the strings are set in motion identify the three families within the string group. First, there are the instruments played by drawing a bow across the surface of the string, as the violin, viola, cello and double bass. Second, there are strings which are struck by hammers, as in the case of the piano. Third, the strings are plucked with the fingers, as in the case of the harp or guitar, or with a mechanical device, as in the case of the mandolin. Now let's discuss each group.

The Bowed Strings. Drawing a bow across the stretched strings results in vibrations which produce tones. Different pitches are obtained by pressing the fingers of the left hand against the strings to change the length of the vibrating section of the string. The longer the string, the lower the pitch; the shorter the string, the higher the tone.

The lute was one of the very earliest string instruments and is a direct ancestor of the violin. Many centuries ago the lute was similar to our present-day guitar. It had a pear-shaped body and six to thirteen strings, which were plucked with the fingers. People began to draw archer's bows across the strings, which produced an odd sort of scraping sound. From this rather humble and unpromising start, craftsmen developed a group of instruments known as *viols*, improving the construction, developing bows and strings and wooden boxes, which when played properly, would emit a sweet and pleasant sound. Gradually, groups of musicians came together to play and sing, and the viols, now made in different sizes, would often be assigned to play the melody. The small ones could be played resting in the player's lap, or tucked between neck and shoulder; the larger ones would rest on the floor. These viols developed into the present-day family of four-string instruments in common use; the violins, or the soprano voice; the violas, or alto voice; the violoncellos (or just cellos), the tenor voice; and the double basses, the bass voice. All four of these instruments are used in the orchestra. In fact, the string section is considered the real backbone of any orchestra. String ensembles are also important and many composers, both past and present, have written music for various combinations of strings. Perhaps the most frequent is the string quartet—two violins, a viola and a cello. Some of the world's most sublime music has been composed for this grouping.

The violin. Perhaps the most important instrument of the orchestra; the violin has a most expressive quality, can be both delicate and brilliant in sound and has enormous range and flexibility. No wonder it has been a favorite instrument of many composers. Violins are made of about sixty different pieces of wood. There are four strings, which are tuned in fifths, from G (the lowest string) to D to A to E. The bow used is slightly curved and is generally strung with horsehair. A substance called rosin is rubbed on the hairs so the bow will "grip" the strings properly. The player nestles the instrument under the chin and against the neck and shoulder and draws the bow with the right hand. Left-hander and right-hander play the violin alike.

The viola. Similar in appearance to the violin and played in the same fashion, it is slightly larger and is able to play lower tones. It has a full and sono-

All four string instruments are manufactured in graded sizes. This young musician is playing on her three-quarter size violin.

rous sound. Its strings are slightly thicker than those of the violin and are tuned from C to G to D to A. The bow used is a bit heavier than the violin bow and is not quite as flexible.

For many years the viola was used solely to strengthen the lower sonorities of the orchestra and to carry the inner harmonies, but it is now given important melodies and passages to play. It is also used as an independent solo instrument and, of course, is one of the mainstays of any string quartet.

The violoncello. Usually known as the cello, its principal predecessor was the viola da gamba, a member of the viol family that had six strings and was sometimes called a "knee fiddle." These precursors of the modern cello still crop up occasionally when a baroque ensemble is performing in the manner of the time, but the viola da gamba is a rarity today and is not used at all in the modern orchestra.

Some say that the cello is the instrumental voice closest to the human voice. Its rich, mellow tones are ideally suited for solo playing and make it an important orchestral and chamber ensemble member. It is available in several sizes for the young student.

Today's cello has a very wide range. It can play tones lower than the viola and is also capable of producing very brilliant and beautiful high tones. The strings are thicker and about twice as long as those of the violin. The bow is shorter, heavier and not as flexible as a violin bow. Cello strings are tuned an octave below the viola, the lowest is C, then G, D and A. The cello is not as agile or brilliant as the violin, but it has an extremely mellow and full tone. Many people feel that of all the instruments, its "voice" comes closest to the human voice.

The double bass or as it is sometimes called, the bass violin resembles the three-string bass viol of the early family of viols. Its name comes from the fact that it was originally used to "double" or play the same part as the cello, but an octave lower. The instrument has the deepest voice of any of the strings and many composers use it to provide a resonant bass sound that is so important and satisfying in many orchestral settings.

The instrument is not as flexible as the other strings and does not lend itself to solo performance. There are a few musical rarities calling for a solo double bass, but the instrument has become very popular in both the modern dance band and in many jazz combinations. Here it is frequently played pizzicato (the strings are plucked with the fingers) rather than being bowed. The strings of the double bass are tuned in fourths: E, A, D and G. Occasionally an attachment is added to provide even lower tones.

Choosing a String Instrument

Most string players usually begin on either the violin or the cello because there is a vast musical literature for these instruments as solo voices or accompanied by just the piano. Once launched on either of these two fine solo and orchestral instruments, players can switch quite readily to either viola or double bass. In most cases cello players switch to the bass and violinists take up the viola. Generally this happens because of the desire to join an orchestra or other instrumental ensemble.

All four of the string instruments have roughly the same problems to be overcome and call for the same basic techniques. Incidentally, all four are now manufactured in graded sizes so young beginners can be started on small-size instruments and gradually brought along to handle the full-size instrument. There is a further discussion of this in Chapter 5.

Now, what are the special qualities which a natural string player has? What sort of youngster is best suited to one of the strings? First, string players need good ears—they must almost "feel" through their ears, a smooth and pleasant tone quality, and they require a naturally acute ability to differentiate pitch. The latter—to be able to judge the quality of a tone made when the bow is drawn across a string, as well as the precise pitch of that tone—is a key factor for a string player. Although a student with limited natural aptitude can be taught a great deal, and continued playing and exposure will sharpen anyone in these areas, natural endowment plays an important role here. The best potential string player must have some natural ability to combine a good ear with good motor control of the arms, shoulders, hands, wrists and fingers.

How can you tell if your child has these attributes in sufficient quantity and quality to make him "a natural" for a string instrument? Well, he is likely to be the type of youngster who will wince upon hearing an out-of-tune piano, or who will make a comment if someone in the family sings "out of tune." He's a child who has an ear for sounds of all kinds and shows that he is alert to the differences in pitch and quality of sounds. These abilities usually have a high degree of correlation with the capacity for repeating given pitches with great accuracy. Perhaps you have noticed that some children can hum back a tune or even a disconnected series of notes played on a piano or other instrument. They do so almost automatically, without thinking or preparing, and they can do it remarkably well. That is, the voice can accurately repeat the notes which the ear took in; the brain can transmit the heard information to a voice box which can reproduce it. Quite an amazing process and even more so for those who can do it "right on the button."

For such gifted youngsters, string instruments can be a great pleasure. But there are other factors to consider, too. For the violin and viola, the beginning player needs plenty of good old-fashioned muscular stamina. When played, the instruments are supported entirely by the player. He also has to assume some body positions (the bend of the left wrist around the neck of the instrument, for example) that are in no way natural. Some young beginners find these so difficult to overcome that they are never able to make satisfactory progress. But this necessary physical stamina can be developed with practice, as long as the child wants to do it.

A certain coordination is also helpful. Each of the four string instruments we've been talking about demands that the player make a certain movement with the left hand and a different series of movements with the right hand and arm. Think for a moment of patting the stomach with the right hand

and rubbing the top of your head with the left—simultaneously. Some people are quick to "catch on" to this exercise; others find it quite difficult. Those children who are good at such tricks overcome the coordination problems of the bowed strings more rapidly.

Some people have advanced the theory that a left-handed person has a natural advantage on a string. Since the fine finger movements are made with the left hand on all bowed strings, it may be helpful, though there are no scientific studies one may fall back on to "prove" it. Both right- and left-handed people can play a string instrument well.

There is one other key factor for rating a potentially good string player. There is no doubt that the string instruments require the greatest amount of patience from the beginner. The time before the student can be expected to make any reasonably satisfying sounds is the greatest compared to any of the other instruments. Satisfaction that one is "making music" must be postponed until certain technical difficulties have been surmounted. The student who moves slowly, or who must win great success early, is not likely to be happy with the strings. With the single exception of the piano, the strings require the longest course of technical study for any degree of real mastery. And the piano can provide many more temporary satisfactions along the way.

Most string players—as is the case for almost everything else—are made, not born. So, don't feel that your child has to be the ideal or else be denied the right to study a string. Natural desire, a decent ear, reasonable coordination and the willingness to persevere are the makings. Anything above that is to be considered a "bonus."

Oh, yes, there is one other factor. Perhaps it is a

small one, but in many households it becomes important. The first number of weeks, or even months, find the beginning string player making sounds that are likely to draw neighboring cats and dogs. These less than completely satisfactory sounds need to be tolerated with understanding and humor by both the player and by anyone within earshot of his practicing. If one can "serve" a certain amount of time, one can be treated to some of the most beautiful and moving sounds that man has been able to create. In short, the apprenticeship can be longer, and, in certain ways, more painful than it is on most other instruments; the rewards can be plentiful.

The Plucked Strings

The instruments in this section don't have the same kind of family grouping that the bowed strings have. In fact, the instruments that are most important here have very little superficial resemblance to one another. The basic technique means that the strings of these instruments are plucked, either with the fingers or with a plectrum, a small hand-held pick.

The harp. This is probably the oldest of the string instruments. Pictures of bow-shaped harps can be found on three-thousand-year-old wall paintings in Egypt. Triangular harps are shown on vase paintings of the ancient Greeks. Of course the harp is the instrument most frequently mentioned in the Old Testament; it was very closely associated with the reciting and singing of the psalms.

Originally, each string of the harp produced a single tone. Much later, a pedal was introduced which made it possible to change the lengths of the strings. With these pedals, the concert harp can play any major or minor scale.

The modern harp has forty-seven strings and seven pedals. Since the strings are placed quite close together, they are color-keyed so the performer can easily locate the proper strings. Only four fingers of each hand are used to pluck the strings (the little finger does not do any plucking). The harp is both a solo and an accompaniment instrument. It is particularly effective in an orchestral setting when played with the woodwinds.

The harp is a complicated and difficult instrument. It requires many of the same natural aptitudes as the piano. The student should have well-developed two-hand coordination and good foot-hand coordination in order to handle the pedaling. He must also have good eye-hand coordination. A successful harpist must be a serious student who will be willing to persist through the difficult and sometimes unrewarding early stages.

There are no special anatomical requirements for a harpist. A keen sense of hearing is important, however, because a harpist must ultimately learn to tune his own instrument properly.

For some reason, it became traditional for young women to be trained as harpists. During the Victorian era, harp was considered excellent training for "young ladies of good breeding." And so "society" produced many fine harpists who, before the days of Women's Lib, were usually the only females to be found in an orchestra pit. Even today, one will frequently find a female playing the harp in a symphony orchestra. But there is nothing sissyish about the harp.

It should be mentioned that the harp is a very expensive instrument. No one except the most serious and determined young person should take it on. Since the player usually is required to bring his own instrument when playing with an orchestra, there is the additional problem of the transportation, storage and care of a large instrument in a large case that cannot be readily carted around in the family Volkswagen.

If the student and his family are willing to overcome all these basic difficulties, the study of the harp can be exciting and rewarding.

The guitar. This most important and certainly most popular of the "plectrum" instruments is part of the group that includes the mandolin, banjo and ukulele. The guitar is a valuable instrument for self-accompaniment for the voice student or folk singer, but it has also come back into vogue as a solo instrument. In fact, there has been a phenomenal rise in interest in guitar playing during the past decade or so, and it shows no signs of abating.

There are three different styles of guitar playing. Each has its own techniques and skills. The most common and easiest to learn is basic folk guitar.

The guitar is the most popular of the plectrum instruments. It is a valuable instrument for self-accompaniment for the voice student or folk singer.

Here the guitar is used as a chordal accompaniment instrument to singing. It is relatively simple for a student who has received a basic musical training on one of the common orchestral instruments, or on piano, to learn some folk guitar by himself with the help of a good method book. Therefore, the guitar is strongly recommended as a *second instrument* rather than as a starting instrument for the young student. It offers a more limiting musical experience, since guitar is not commonly used in either an orchestra, a band or a chamber ensemble.

The other two styles of guitar playing are classical guitar and Flamenco guitar. Classical guitar does not refer to the playing of music from the classical period; it refers, rather, to playing the solo music composed for the guitar. It includes music that has been transcribed for guitar from original lute, harpsichord or other instrumental music.

The Flamenco guitar, although now thought of as a solo style, was originally an accompaniment instrument for a Flamenco singer and dancer. The music is highly emotional and expressive. Traditionally, Flamenco guitar playing was passed on from one person to another. Very little Flamenco music is published or even written down. The solo Flamenco player today, therefore, requires a good teacher whom he can copy, much like the pupils of old finding a master with whom they could learn and to whom they became apprenticed. Today's student, however, has an advantage in that many good recordings are available. A solo performer creates his pieces by drawing from the improvisation of past performers and by adding his own original settings while sticking to the very formal rules of the style.

Both Flamenco and classical guitar playing involve very formal and exacting technical style, whereas folk guitar is far more flexible and simpler to learn by ear or by rote, without an extensive knowledge of the language of music.

In general, the guitar student should have a good ear for pitch, since he must be able to learn to tune his own instrument. A folk guitar player should have a good ear for harmony because he must be able to hear and respond properly to the chord changes in a song.

The Flamenco guitar student must also have a creative flair in order to be able to produce well-organized improvisations. His ear for harmony, melodic line and complex rhythmic patterns must be very keen in order to imitate the complicated style.

It might also be mentioned that electric guitar players usually start by learning simple guitar. There are no special anatomical requirements or hazards. Actually, in many ways, the guitar is the "people's instrument," relatively easy to play, quite inexpensive—compared to most other instruments—and a source of great pleasure and delight as a strum-along instrument in countless schools, homes and gatherings around the world.

The Struck Strings

The pianoforte. (Yes, it actually does mean soft-loud, for reasons we will see in a moment.) This is an instrument whose stretched strings are set in vibration by means of hammers. Since it is the most common and most important of the keyboard instruments, it will be used here to represent the entire family, including organ, harpsichord, harmonium, celeste and others. Although all the instruments in the family are not "struck strings" in their method of tone production, they all require very much the same aptitudes. It is strongly recommended that any student wishing to play any keyboard instrument begin by first becoming familiar with and relatively proficient on the piano. Actually, the modern piano is a fairly recent development. The first public recital on the pianoforte was not given until J. C. Bach, youngest son of Johann Sebastian Bach, performed on the instrument in London in 1768. It was some sixty years after the introduction of the instrument by its inventor, a harpsichord builder named Bartolomeo Cristofori of Florence, Italy. The instrument he devised was superior to the widely used harpsichord because it was capable of producing loud and soft sound with a great deal of dynamic range and could "take" considerably more force than the far more delicate clavichord. Perhaps you have heard the marvelous harpsichord sound. Although extremely well-suited to much of the music composed for it, the harpsichord is a limited instrument. It does not have a great deal of flexibility and the sound produced does not have a wide range of sonorities. The pianoforte, on the other hand, can go from a whispered pianissimo to the thundering climaxes of a fortissimo. In little more than two hundred and fifty years, the piano has become the undisputed king of instruments, the "compleat instrument," if you will, and the one that all musicians, amateur and professional alike, consider the basic instrument for the study of music. Since its first appearance, the basic design has remained virtually unchanged. Refinements have wrought an instrument that not only can last over several lifetimes of continuous play but has a range and richness of expression, a beauty of shape and style and a literature unmatched by any other instrument.

What does it take to become a pianist? Can anybody play the piano? What sort of youngster is most likely to succeed and develop a lifetime attachment to the piano? First, let us explode some of the more common myths and preconceptions. Many people have been led to believe that good pianists must have unusually large hands, with a great reach from thumb to pinky when spread-eagled. This is simply not the case. Many great pianists have unusually well-developed hands from many years spent in practice. But there are also many noted pianists who have perfectly "ordinary" hands. There is a tremendous variation in the structure of "pianists' hands." Size, shape, length of fingers and overall structure matter far less than the fashion in which the hands are trained to work, both separately and together. Indeed, there are no other anatomical characteristics that seem to be common to fine pianists.

Another misconception is that the piano student who is all thumbs will never be able to master the instrument. Often, the piano is the best instrument for certain awkward youngsters because it offers a precision in terms of the location of the notes and the spatial absolutes by which everything is laid out. This factor can sometimes help orient an ungainly young player who will make better progress than on a string instrument where an ear-touch sensitivity needs to be developed.

One of the greatest advantages for the beginning piano student lies in the fact that the piano does not require a particularly well-developed ear. Since its tone-quality and the specific pitch is actually "built-in," the player does not have any control over these factors and need not have special concern about them at the beginning of piano study.

Once a piano is properly tuned, it will, all things being equal, hold that tune for some time. In any event, the player is not responsible for tuning the instrument and there is less worry and fuss over this element than with any of the other instruments. This whole area of concern, in other words, need not trouble the beginning pianist or members of his family. If you hit the right key, the right note will play. It is as simple as that. Now, what are some of the complications?

There are two areas of physical gifts which a fortunate piano student will possess in good quantity. They are a good sense of spatial relations and a healthy capacity to acquire certain specific movements of the hands, fingers and arms. Spatial relations mean that the child can readily visualize the distance between two points in front of him. The capacity to coordinate movements means that the child can immediately sense the most efficient way to manipulate his hands and fingers so that they accomplish a series of specific moves. It's hard to pin down better than that. Some people just seem to have a natural ability to move and to coordinate their movements efficiently. Without any training or specific practice, they can immediately make the proper movements, while other people must learn to make these by practicing until they "come naturally." In any event, if your child is well coordinated in finger and hand movements, he will have a good start on the piano. Those youngsters who learned to eat with a knife and fork early and easily are likely to find "two hands at the piano" relatively easy too.

Piano music, in which many notes are played simultaneously, asks that the student be able to visualize several "lines" of music at once. The pianist's eye has to be able to take in these lines and make the necessary transfer to the fingers, which have to move in the required manner. This process is peculiar to the piano; it requires that the pianist synchronize many different things at just the right times. It takes a certain "quickness," a certain automatic kind of movement and eye-hand coordination which some people seem to have naturally. Those people are especially well suited to the piano. Pianists must also have good hand-foot coordination in order to be able to pedal properly.

There are times when determination, a talent for overlooking the frustrations of the moment and keeping one's spirits up by thinking of future rewards, can be more important than all the physical talents. With that sort of courage many people of limited talent have succeeded far beyond others and far beyond the goals that may have been predicted by pessimistic parents and dubious teachers. Old-fashioned desire can overcome most handicaps. So don't be afraid to give your child a chance at the piano if he wants it.

While the piano has a very limited use in the orchestra (as part of the orchestral ensemble) and is not used at all in school bands, it does have the largest and richest solo and chamber repertoire of all the instruments. It offers endless opportunities for performance as a solo instrument, an ensemble instrument and an accompanying instrument for voice and virtually all other instruments.

It is the only instrument (other keyboard instruments also are included here) that offers the player the opportunity to make unaccompanied music in an endless and always satisfying variety. The piano, in effect, accompanies itself, for it can play with a "completeness" possessed by no other instrument. With all the other instruments, sooner or later one must play in an ensemble of some sort; there is a limit to what the unaccompanied string, brass, woodwind or percussion instrument can do. But not the piano—it is king in this respect. It is the basic instrument for all those who have professional goals and wish to study music seriously. All professional musicians should have a more than passing acquaintance with the piano. The study of music, including harmony, theory, counterpoint and composition, requires a familiarity with the piano. In fact, a lack of sufficient piano technique can be a serious handicap to most people who wish to have a career in music (see Chapter 7).

The Wind Instruments

There are two subdivisions of wind instruments: the woodwinds and the brasses. In order to produce a sound on any of these instruments, the air column must be forced to vibrate. The manner in which this is accomplished provides us with a simple method of classifying the wind instruments into smaller families.

Flute-type instruments are called air-reeds. With this method of tone production, the air stream is directed from the player's lips across a circular hole bored in the pipe. The wind stream strikes the sharp edge of the hole on the side farthest from the player's mouth. Think of the sound you produce when you blow across the top of a soda bottle. If you've done that, then you've played an air-reed instrument!

Clarinet-type instruments, including saxophones, are called single-reeds. The player's breath sets in motion a single reed which vibrates against the opening in the instrument's mouthpiece.

Oboe-type instruments, including English horn and bassoon, are called double-reeds. The opening between the two pieces of cane is quite small. The player takes the two reeds between his lips and the pressure of his breath and lips forces the two reeds to vibrate. These double-reed instruments do not have a mouthpiece.

The brass family, including trumpet, French horn, trombone and tuba, are called lip-reeds. These instruments are made of metal tubes with a mouthpiece, usually of metal, at the upper end of the tube. (Some instrument makers are now experimenting with fiber glass in the manufacture of previously all metal "brasses.") The player's lips stretch across the mouthpiece and themselves act as the vibrating reeds.

There are many parents, as well as physicians and dentists, who have misconceptions about wind instruments and the effect that playing them has on the human body. We hear many "rumors" about wind instruments requiring an enormous lung capacity, and other instruments being dangerous to the heart of a young child. And a great deal of misinformation is passed on about the effect of certain instruments on children and their growing teeth. Let us discuss each of these areas and try to dispel some of the myths that seem to have become "facts."

Myth: Playing certain winds requires a tremendous lung capacity and great respiratory strength. *Fact:* Wind playing does not require such special capacities. In fact, practice on wind instruments has been used with considerable success in the treatment of certain respiratory weaknesses and with children who suffer asthmatic conditions. A doctor with *specific* experience and knowledge of the requirements of the instrument should consult with the parents and music teacher to make a determination for a particular case.

Myth: Playing a trumpet or an oboe or one of the

other winds can put an abnormal stress on the heart. *Fact:* Wind playing does not put any unusual stress on the heart of a normal child, though some children will pant and become out of breath easily at the beginning of their course of study, before they have mastered some of the important breathing techniques involved. If a child suffers from a cardiac abnormality, then obviously caution is required. At the beginning stages of studying certain instruments, there is a good bit of exertion involved. Special children should consult with their prospective teacher and doctor before committing themselves to a particular instrument.

Myth: Playing a wind instrument malforms the lips. *Fact:* No harm is done to the lips by playing a wind instrument. The lips gain a high degree of muscle tone and strength by practice on a wind instrument, but no new muscle tissue is created and nothing is destroyed.

Myth: A child whose teeth are still growing and developing should avoid playing a wind instrument. *Fact:* We probably should say *facts* here because this is the area with the greatest number of misconceptions, and in which the largest number of false starts and difficulties lie. During certain types of orthodontic treatment, the practice of wind instruments can actually be of positive help because of the position in which the instruments are held when played. For example, if a child wears braces because of protruding upper teeth, his condition may be helped by practice on a trumpet, trombone, tuba or French horn. The playing of a single-reed instrument, such as clarinet or saxophone, can help correct a condition of lower-jaw protrusion.

It is also true that playing a clarinet will be detrimental to some mouth and teeth conditions, as will the playing of some of the other winds. If your child wears braces or you know that he will be starting treatment with braces in the future, it is advisable to consult your orthodontist or family dentist first—before an instrument is chosen for study. It is unfair to let a child get off to a good start on an instrument that he enjoys, only to tell him a year later that he must give it up because of necessary dental work. Most orthodontists will allow a patient to play almost any instrument, if the daily practice time is relatively short. A half hour or an hour a day of instrumental practice will not usually interfere with the twenty-four-hour-a-day influence of braces.

Unless the dentist you use is familiar with the wide variety of mouth positions involved in playing various wind instruments, it would be best if decisions could be made jointly by the dentist and the school or private music teacher who can be expected to make you, the parent, the best recommendation.

A final *fact:* It is important to understand that, while certain wind instruments are helpful in correcting certain orthodontal problems and other instruments will act as impediments to proper orthodonture, no wind instrument will do any damage at all to a normal mouth either in appearance or in function.

The flute and the piccolo. The flute is a very old instrument and therefore has a very large and comprehensive solo and chamber repertoire awaiting the player. The flute is a very important instrument in both orchestras and bands. In recent years the flute has also gained prominence in Latin American music as well as in modern jazz groups. The flute is a soprano instrument which is very

Tone is produced on the flute by blowing across a hole in the mouthpiece.

agile (it has a great range and can be played accurately very fast), so it is no wonder that the instrument is so popular today. And because its literature is so large and varied, coming from virtually every period in which music was written, there is an endless supply of material for the performer.

The piccolo is smaller than the flute and sounds one octave higher. This "little brother" is used in bands and orchestras for very high passage work. It is a sort of specialty instrument which a flute player can easily learn to double on.

Tone is produced on both flute and piccolo by blowing across a hole in the mouthpiece. Both instruments have cylindrical bores and are almost identical in fingering. Higher and lower tones are produced by opening and closing tone holes along the length of the instrument, thus making the cylinder longer or shorter.

The range of the flute is three octaves, from middle C to the second C above the treble staff. The flute is made up of three pieces, or joints:

1. *the headpiece*, which contains the blowing hole
2. *the body*, which is a long joint with holes and keys
3. *the foot joint*, or *tail*, which also has keys and holes

Most flutes are made either of silver or nickel-silver plate or cocuswood. Some flutes are made of gold. The wooden flutes tend to have a more mellow tone; metal flutes tend to sound more brilliant. The player's lips act as the vibrating reed.

The student who chooses the flute should be able to produce a tone on the blowing hole of the headpiece alone. After a very brief instruction, some students will find this form of tone production quite natural and easy. It is similar to blowing across the top of a bottle and getting a nice rich, mellow sound. The certain way you have to place your lips is called the embouchure. Of course, every wind instrument demands a slightly different embouchure. Not everyone finds them equally easy—or difficult.

Some beginners experience a slight lightheadedness or dizziness when they make their first attempts to play the flute. This is quite natural, since they usually waste a great deal of air "trying too hard." Actually, very little air is necessary—the direction and control of the air being blown are what really count. But it takes most beginners a while to adjust, and this means an occasional bout of feeling dizzy for some. Nothing to worry about. Few flutists have a recurrence after the first several lessons!

In addition to aptitude for tone production on an

"air-reed," a student should be able to hold the instrument in its correct horizontal position. The student's arms must be strong enough and long enough to reach the finger positions while supporting the weight of the instrument. A flute player also needs good finger dexterity and coordination. While a good sense of hearing for both pitch and tonal quality is essential for the advanced flute player, this particular aptitude is not as vital a prerequisite for flute study as it is for the strings. In fact, flute is a relatively easy instrument in the early stages and does not require the same perseverance and stamina that piano or string study demands of the beginner.

One other word about the flute. For some reason, playing this instrument is still associated in the minds of some folks with the tea salon filled with ladies listening to ladies playing the flute. There are still people who feel it is a "girl's instrument." That is, of course, complete nonsense. There is nothing sissyish about the flute (or about any other instrument, for that matter) and it is a perfectly appropriate instrument for a young man to learn.

It might also be noted that the flute has one great advantage. It is lightweight, and easy to carry about and handle. For the handicapped child who may have certain motor disabilities, the flute can be a fine choice.

The clarinet. This is a descendant of a medieval instrument known as the "chalumeau," a small cylindrical pipe. It had no "bell" at the end but was played with a single beating reed which was similar to the modern clarinet reed.

The modern clarinet is a cylindrical pipe of wood, ebonite or metal, and is about two feet in length. Its sections from top to bottom are called:

1. *the mouthpiece*
2. *the barrel-joint*
3. *the left-hand* or *top joint*
4. *the right-hand* or *lower joint*
5. *the bell*

All the holes, keys and rings are contained on the left- and right-hand joints. The mouthpiece is usually made of wood, hard rubber or crystal. The upper part of the "beak" mouthpiece is flattened to form the "table" which supports the reed. The reed is a single piece of carefully prepared cane. Tone is produced when the player sets the reed vibrating by blowing between the reed and the table of the mouthpiece. This sets the air column in motion inside the instrument. The reed was originally bound to the table of the mouthpiece by fine twine, but today it is secured in place with a metal "ligature."

During the classical period, orchestral clarinets

The clarinet is a single reed instrument with a large range and great versatility.

were made in three keys: C, B-flat and A. The C clarinet is now obsolete. The written range of both the B-flat and the A clarinet is from E below the treble staff to the second A above the treble staff. The two instruments are fingered identically and differ only in that the A clarinet is about an inch longer than the B-flat clarinet and sounds a half step lower.

The bass clarinet. Pitched an octave below the standard clarinet, it is used both in bands and in orchestras and is quite a bit larger than the regular instrument. There is also a small *E-flat clarinet* in the family which is used regularly in bands and only occasionally in the orchestra. The *alto clarinet* is the tenor member of the family. All these instruments have the same fingering and require the same technique. It is quite simple for a clarinetist to play them all after he becomes proficient on the standard B-flat instrument.

There is a large literature written for the clarinet, which is a basic member of both the band and orchestra. In the concert band, it plays the role of the violin. It has great technical flexibility, a great variety in tonal color and a large dynamic range. Oddly enough, though it sprang from an ancient form of instrument, the clarinet didn't become mechanically perfected until the eighteenth century. It was Mozart who first recognized its possibilities and wrote extensively for it as a solo instrument and as an important instrument in his orchestra. So, the clarinet repertoire is lacking prior to the classical period. However, from that time forward, it was written for as a solo instrument and as an ensemble instrument in various chamber combinations, in addition to becoming an important orchestra and band instrument.

The clarinet was also discovered to be an ideal

instrument for the rhythm and flexibility involved in jazz. It was an essential instrument in the old street parades, the Dixieland jazz band, and later in progressive and modern jazz.

The B-flat clarinet is the best single-reed instrument for the beginner. Not only does it have the largest musical literature, it is also able to fit into numerous ensemble situations and can be played in a wide variety of styles to suit virtually any temperament. It is simple for a clarinet player to switch to saxophone later in the game, because the techniques and the fingerings are quite similar.

The clarinet is also somewhat easier to hold for the young student than the flute because the clarinet is held straight down in front of the body with most of the weight resting on the right thumb. The arms are down in a very natural position. The beginning student should have hands and fingers large enough to cover the holes and keys comfortably.

The clarinet is a good choice for the child who is unsure of his musical gifts. There is a certain amount of frustration in producing a good tone at the beginning. Considerable care in putting the instrument together properly must be learned, for the pieces fit together in one particular way. The major problem to overcome with the clarinet is in the use of the reed. This small piece of shaved cane must be changed from time to time. Even the best reed is rendered unusable after a certain amount of playing, just as a razor blade must be changed, no matter how tough the blade or how expert the shaver. Since no two reeds are alike, and different players require different kinds of reeds, the beginning clarinetist (in fact, all clarinetists, even the most expert) must get used to "tinkering" with and changing reeds to get the best sound. It takes a little getting used to, that's all.

The clarinet is an instrument which demands relatively little of the beginner, produces music with a modest investment of time and study, and requires no special physical aptitudes other than good finger coordination and dexterity. It is no wonder that each year a great many students begin their music study on the clarinet and then rapidly become members of a band, orchestra or ensemble group. Generally, any student with the true desire to succeed on the clarinet will be able to do so.

The Saxophone Family

The saxophone. This is a kind of cross between the woodwind family and the brass family. The mouthpiece used is a single reed, just like that of the clarinet, but the body of the instrument is a conical brass tube. The source of vibration is the single reed, when the player blows air between it and the tip of the mouthpiece.

The saxophone is a relatively modern offshoot of the clarinet. It is considered part of the woodwind family even though it is made of metal. (Courtesy The Selmer Company.)

The saxophone is made up of the straight and curved *B-flat sopranos*, the *E-flat alto*, the *C melody*, *B-flat tenor*, *E-flat baritone* and *B-flat bass*. The three most popular models are the alto, tenor and baritone. The saxophone technique is relatively easy compared to that of other woodwind instruments. The range, technique and notation for the entire family are practically identical. The range is from B-natural below the treble staff to E-flat above the treble staff. Scales, arpeggios and florid figures are quite easily played on the saxophone.

Because it is a relatively new instrument, the saxophone solo and chamber repertoire is rather limited. However, the instrument is coming into its own and composers today are treating it as a serious solo and ensemble instrument. It plays a very important role in bands, but is only occasionally used in orchestras. Of course, its main use has been as a jazz instrument. Its mournful, wailing tone, its flexibility and the relative ease of fingering make it a fine instrument for improvisation, the essence of its use in jazz. Its particularly distinctive tone-quality has also fostered its wide use in pop music and as part of the standard instrumentation in the big-band sound.

The saxophone requires roughly the same aptitudes as the clarinet. For that reason, it is often recommended that a student begin on clarinet and later transfer to, or double, on the saxophone. Flute-players frequently double on the saxophone because there is great similarity in the fingering of the two instruments.

The oboe and the English horn. The oboe is a double-reed instrument. Its immediate parent was the Discant-Schalmey from which it developed in the last quarter of the seventeenth century. It is made of a small, conically bored pipe using cocus-wood, rosewood or ebonite. At its lower end is a

The oboe, a double reed instrument, is more difficult for beginners than either the clarinet or flute.

bell; at its upper end is a short length of metal tubing called the "staple" into which the double reed is fitted. This double reed is made of two extremely fine and thin pieces of prepared cane which are bound together. These are caused to vibrate when the player forces air between them. As with the flute, the notes are produced by opening or closing the holes along the tubing in certain patterns. The oboe is built in the key of C and has a range from B-flat below the treble clef to G four lines above.

Physical aptitude for the oboe includes excellent motor control of the fingers for both coordination and dexterity, as well as the capacity for subtle breath and lip control. The oboe requires only a minimal amount of breath, but the player must learn to control his breath intake and allow only a small stream of air to enter the instrument through the vibrating double reed. To do this well is admittedly difficult. It takes much longer for a beginning oboist to produce a satisfying sound than it does for a flute or clarinet beginner. The oboe player must also possess a fine sensitivity to tone-quality. So, we can see that the oboist must be willing to persevere through the less satisfying early stages, much like the string player.

An oboist has an endless variety of solo, ensemble and orchestra music at his disposal. The oboe is such an old instrument that its music spans all the periods. It is also an important member of the symphonic band of today. Since really good oboists are scarce, a player of any skill is almost guaranteed a job, and a competent amateur will surely be sought after by community orchestras and chamber groups. But it should also be mentioned that the oboe is not a particularly flexible instrument; little use is made of it in pop music or in jazz. Since it takes a good bit of time to learn to play it well, usually only the most serious and dedicated student with particularly well-defined goals will embark on the oboe.

The English horn. It is neither English nor a horn! It should simply be thought of as a contralto oboe. Its wooden pipe is wider and longer than that of the oboe, and it ends in a small globular bell. At the upper end, the metal crook or staple which holds the double reed is generally bent back at an angle to the pipe itself. The reed is larger and thicker than the oboe reed. The English horn is built to sound a perfect fifth below the oboe and its fingering is almost the same as that for the oboe. So it is easy for an oboe player to double on or switch completely to English horn, after first becoming proficient on the oboe.

The bassoon. This instrument's history began in the sixteenth century: it developed from the old Bass-Pommer, which was the true bass of the Schalmey family (the same family of instruments

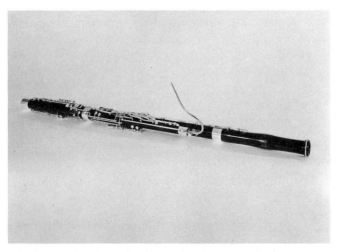

The bassoon is a large double reed instrument. It plays an important role in bands and orchestras. (Courtesy of The Selmer Company.)

from which the oboe descended). The bassoon is also a double-reed instrument with a conical bore and it is the bass voice for the double-reed choir. Vibrations are generated as they are in the oboe, when air is forced through the double-reed, which is larger than that of either the oboe or the English horn.

The bassoon pipe is doubled back upon itself to reduce its length to about four feet. The whole pipe is divided into five pieces which are, from the top down:

1. *the crook*, a narrow, curved tube of metal to which the double reed is attached
2. *the wing*
3. the *double joint* at the lower end of which the pipes meet and reverse their direction
4. *the long* or *bass joint*, which lies next to and extends upward beyond the wing
5. *the bell*

The instrument is held diagonally by the player. The bell points upward to his left hand and the double joint comes down to his right side.

The range of the bassoon is unusually large. It goes from B-flat, third space below the bass clef, to G-sharp, first space above the treble clef, a range of almost four octaves.

The bassoon is an important member of both the band and orchestra. Its solo and chamber literature is somewhat limited, however.

The double bassoon or contrabassoon. This instrument, which sounds one octave lower than the regular bassoon, plays a very limited role in both band and orchestra.

The regular bassoon is a large, heavy instrument and is not recommended for the young beginner. The student must be strong enough to carry the instrument and his hands must be large enough to reach the finger positions. Bassoonists often begin their instrumental training on the clarinet or saxophone and then switch when they are physically mature and wish to work hard on a special instrument which, though its rewards are more limited than some of the more "popular" instruments, is nevertheless an important and richly satisfying one.

It is well to mention at this point that choosing an oboe, English horn or bassoon means starting a costly undertaking. These instruments are not only expensive to purchase but also expensive to maintain (see Chapter 5).

The Brass Instruments

Brass instruments date back to antiquity. Their original form was undoubtedly an animal's horn or tusk with a cup-shaped mouthpiece at the smaller end. Later they were just plain tubes, straight or curved. Eventually, holes were pierced in the tubing and keys were added. But it wasn't until the piston valve was invented in 1815 that the trumpet assumed its present form.

The trumpet. The tubing is approximately cylindrical in two-thirds of its length and conical in one-third, and like that of most of the brass instruments, is bent and circled back on itself many times in order to make the instrument easier to hold. Its sound is made by the vibration of the player's lips stretched across a cup-like mouthpiece. Different pitches are produced when the player tightens or loosens his lips. The trumpet has three valves, which enable it to produce the full chromatic scale. The first valve serves to route the air column through a length of tubing adequate to lower the pitch a whole tone. The second valve controls a half tone and the third controls a tone and a half.

The trumpet is usually built in the key of B-flat.

The trumpet is the most popular instrument in the brass family.

Some trumpets are also built in the key of C, so they can be played without the player having to do transposing. The familiar tone of the trumpet is crisp and penetrating. When played softly and expertly, with or without a mute, the trumpet can produce a mournful, eerie, and not unpleasant sound. Its range is from F-sharp below the treble clef to C above.

The trumpet is one of the basic instruments of both band and orchestra; its use in dance bands and as a jazz instrument is known wherever music is played. It is as necessary to a brass ensemble as a violin is to a string quartet. A trumpet player can play from a large literature and in virtually any style or period. The trumpet is a versatile instrument and should be considered the basic beginning instrument of the brass family.

The cornet. Related to the trumpet, it differs mainly in the shape of its tubing. It is more conical than the trumpet, so it has a fuller, more mellow tone. It has the same range and its technique is precisely the same as for the trumpet.

The French horn. Made of very long, small conical tubing, it uses a small, deep mouthpiece. Because its tubing is so narrow, the lower part of its scale is not easily played. The French horn has the largest range of all the brass instruments, three octaves from C, one octave below middle C, to C above the treble clef. Because there are so many open tones that can be produced without the aid of valves, the French-horn player must have an extremely well-trained embouchure and a very keen ear for pitch.

French horns are built either as single or double horns. The double horn has more open tones than the single horn and also has a wider playing range. It makes both the lower and higher notes easier to

The French horn has the largest range of all the brass instruments. (Courtesy The Selmer Company.)

play. Because the French horn requires so much more lip and breath control than the other brass instruments, it is usually advisable for a player to begin on one of the simpler brass instruments and then transfer to French horn after he gets a good foundation.

The French horn has a very large role in both bands and orchestras, and a few French horn players have ventured into the jazz field. Good French-horn players are not common. Anyone with a reasonable mastery of this difficult instrument is in great demand, whether amateur or professional.

The trombone. Cylindrical in two-thirds of its length and conical in the lower third, it ends in a bell, just like the trumpet. But its tubing is twice as long, causing it to sound one octave lower than the trumpet. It is the tenor voice of the brass family. The length of the tubing is changed by moving the slide from closed, or first, position to any one of six

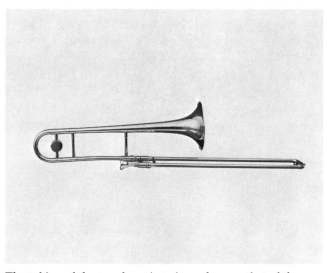

The tubing of the trombone is twice as long as that of the trumpet. (Courtesy The Selmer Company.)

other positions. Each position is located at a fixed distance from the closed position and there are no markings on the slide. The ear and hand of the player must tell him when the correct length of tubing has been added and the right pitch thus produced. In this respect, the trombone requires the same degree of hearing sensitivity as the string instruments. The bore of the trombone is larger than that of the trumpet, as is its mouthpiece, although the shape of the latter is very similar. The valve trombone uses valves instead of a slide, but is like the conventional slide trombone in all other respects. The bass trombone can reach lower notes and is a little heavier, but its playing techniques are the same as those for the regular trombone.

The trombone is an important band and orchestra instrument. Its chamber literature is limited to brass ensembles and its solo literature is small indeed. But the trombone has gained wide use in dance bands—it is vital for that big-band sound. And the trombone has become one of the most important instruments in jazz. The free and easy sliding sounds of the instrument and its rich, deep register are pleasant and familiar to most of us. But to achieve them takes a good bit of control and practice.

The euphonium and the baritone horn. These are the baritone voices of the brass family. They occupy the same position in the band as does the cello in the orchestra. They are lovely harmony and solo instruments with a very mellow tone-quality. The baritone horn is one of the easiest instruments to blow in the entire brass family.

The tuba and the sousaphone. The lowest-sounding members of the brass family, these instruments are about twice the length (in tubing) of the trombone and baritone and about four times the length of the trumpet and cornet. Therefore

The baritone horn is often heard and seen on parade grounds or between halves of a football game. (Courtesy The Selmer Company.)

they sound an octave lower than the trombone and two octaves lower than the trumpet. The large bore and large mouthpiece help produce a deep, rich, organ-like tone. The tuba is important to the orchestra, though it has limited agility and range. It is confined in most band and orchestral repertoires to low-range support and the playing of basic harmony. In fact, the popular song story, "Tubby the Tuba," makes the point that the poor tuba has been longing to play the solo part, the melody, just once!

The sousaphone was specifically designed and shaped so the player could carry and play it while marching in a band. Indeed, it is a staple of the marching bands seen all across the country particularly during the football season.

Though not really part of the training of young musicians, these large brass instruments have special and often exciting uses. But sometimes, when a player switches from trumpet or trombone, he may find a special affinity for one of these large brasses which can lead to a lifetime of happy music-making.

A final few words on the brass family. Trumpet and trombone are certainly the most logical beginning instruments in this group. In addition to a sensitive ear and the ability to produce a good sound on a lip-reed type of mouthpiece, there are some other physical requirements for successful brass playing. A trumpet player must have strong enough arms to hold the instrument straight out in front of his mouth without any other support. A trombonist must have long enough arms to reach the most "far out" slide positions. The trombonist needs the most acute ear of all the brass players because he not only has to choose the correct tone to play in each position, but he must also choose the exact location by the correct placement of his slide.

The French horn requires the most lip control of the brasses, as well as an acute ear. It is usually, but not necessarily, a second instrument after the student has had some experience on trumpet or trombone. Because the tuba is so large and has a limited repertoire, it is not recommended as a beginning instrument. Most students with previous brass training switch over to it easily.

Percussion Instruments

Many people may think that the phrase "percussion instruments" in a book of this kind is a polite way of saying "drums." While it is true that all drums are members of the percussion family, the group also includes those instruments on which the vibrations are set in motion by striking the material of the instrument. The stroke may be made by a hammer or a stick, by the hand of the player or by sections of the instrument hitting against each other.

These percussion instruments can be divided into two basic groups: those which produce sounds without producing a specific pitch, such as the bass drum, snare drum, tambourine, triangle and cymbals; those which can produce differentiated pitches, such as the xylophone, chimes and tympani.

In the world of the professional musician, a percussionist is required to master all the percussion instruments, with the exception of the piano. (As we mentioned before, the piano is a kind of hybrid instrument which can be claimed by both the string and percussion families. You certainly must strike it to play it, but strings produce the sound.) Percussion instruments are not simply for the "nonmusician." They have every bit as much importance as any instrument family. In fact, they probably represent man's most basic and original musical urge—to find expression through rhythm.

The snare drum. The young percussion student is often started on this drum, which comes in many different sizes. It is set up on a small metal stand, as a rule, and is played with two sticks, one in each hand of the player. Often parents become alarmed if they feel they are about to launch a new drummer. They feel that the practice noise might become unbearable. But snare drum students are able to do most of their practicing on a practice pad, a small wooden block mounted with rubber or stretched skin.

The xylophone. This is another basic instrument for the novice percussion player. It is a system of graduated wooden rectangles mounted on a frame—the shorter the wooden strip, the higher Another variety of this instrument is called a *marimba.* Electrified, with metal tubes instead of flat

Two tympani are a regular part of an orchestra's percussion section. The foot pedals are used to adjust the pitch of each drum. (Courtesy The Selmer Company.)

strips, the instrument is called the *vibraharp*! The xylophone is also played with two or more sticks, or mallets. This instrument is used in the orchestra, especially in more contemporary works, and is also used by the concert band. Played on an upright carrying device, the instrument is a familiar aspect of the marching band and is called a glockenspiel.

The successful percussion player has good two-hand motor coordination. And of course, a good sense of rhythm; an ability to count time and meter properly are essential. The visual and spatial sense necessary for the good xylophone player is quite similar to that needed for piano.

While there is some solo enjoyment one can obtain from some of the instruments in the percussion family, most percussion players participate in a variety of different group music-making experiences, from concert orchestra to jazz group. It is not true that only relatively poor musicians "end

A basic stage band drum set includes a bass drum, snare drums and cymbals. (Courtesy The Selmer Company.)

The marimba is one of the most important melody instruments of the percussion family. (Courtesy The Selmer Company.)

up" playing percussion instruments. A truly skill-ful tympanist or xylophone player has often been the result of the same combination of "gift" and hard work that went into producing a skilled clari-netist. A good percussion player is always in de-mand and can find full musical satisfaction. Of course, it is also true that the percussion section of the school band is often an opportunity for a less advanced player to find a role to play in making music. Even the triangle player is participating and must know when to come in and how to strike the instrument to produce the best tone. While no tri-angle player has become a legend, the youngster who plays one in a music group is taking part. And there is always a measure of dignity for anyone who does that.

5

Acquiring and Maintaining an Instrument

Should you rent or buy an instrument for a beginning student? There are psychological as well as financial advantages to renting an instrument in the early stages of instrumental study.

A parent who has not made an enormous financial investment in the purchase of an instrument will be much more willing to accept the fact, after a few months or even a full year, that the child is on the "wrong" instrument. The often-heard parental complaints—"I've spent so much money buying you this beautiful instrument and now you won't even practice"; or "How can you think of switching to another instrument after we've spent so much for this piano?"—would not be spoken if rental were chosen initially over purchase.

The rental money need not be "thrown out" money either. Almost all music stores have arrangements whereby the rental fees can be applied toward the purchase of the instrument at the end of the rental period, assuming the family wishes to buy at that time.

The negative factor in renting rather than purchasing is the quality of the instruments available. Often they are both inferior makes and in poor working condition. When you rent a wind instrument (either brass or woodwind) it is therefore desirable to pay a little bit more and rent a brand-new instrument instead of a used one. The bright and shiny appearance of a new instrument will almost always add excitement and motivation for the young student and you have eliminated the possibility of old and worn mechanisms that will go out of order and need constant repair. You also eliminate the possibility of hidden dents or cracks or leaks which make playing the instrument dramatically more difficult and frustrating. A major cause of first-year dropouts in instrumental study is the discouragement and inconvenience of an instrument that needs frequent repair.

If a new instrument of good quality is rented, it can then be purchased when the family is relatively certain the choice is permanent.

The situation with strings is somewhat more complicated for two reasons. First, violins, violas, cellos and double basses come in many sizes, to fit the young student. Children grow quickly and they change instrument sizes sometimes as frequently as once a year. Second, the quality of string instruments available for rental is usually inferior to the quality of winds and the quantity is often more limited.

It is important to use professional help when renting or buying any musical instrument but it is mandatory when renting or buying a string instrument. Availability and quality will differ from area to area and the child's teacher is the best person to consult. Remember that the child must be measured for correct size, in addition to all the other considerations. There are some music dealers who work out an arrangement whereby a small violin or cello or viola or double bass can be traded in when the child is ready for the next size. If such a dealer does exist in your area, then it might be wise to purchase right from the start, knowing that the instrument will be "bought back" or tradable when the time comes.

Often the public and private schools have instruments which they loan without charge to their students to encourage more young instrumentalists. This is particularly true in the case of the more unusual instruments such as viola, bass violin, French horn, bassoon, oboe, tuba and so on. By providing these instruments free to students, the school insures itself of well-balanced instrumentation in its bands and orchestras.

If the school does not have instruments of its own, it will often make arrangements for students to rent them from a music store. This usually means a slightly lower rental fee, due to the quantity of the business.

When renting or borrowing an instrument, regardless of the source, be sure to inquire about the terms of the rental arrangement for maintenance and repair fees, and about insurance covering such fees, and an all-risk insurance coverage for theft or total loss. Such insurance can be included in the rental fee and can avoid a nasty situation. If a cello falls down a flight of stairs or off a stage and is demolished, it is some comfort to know that insurance will take care of it. If a child leaves his trumpet case on the bus on the way home from a lesson, it is good to know that you do not need to buy the music store a new one! If the music store does not offer such insurance coverage, inquire about getting it from your own broker. It is usually quite inexpensive. This advice applies, quite obviously, to the instrument you own as well as to one you rent.

Sometimes a music store will require a deposit of $10 or more in addition to the rental fee. You get this back at the end of the rental period, provided the instrument is returned in good condition.

Instrumental rental fees are charged by the month or by the school year. Be sure to check on what happens if you return the instrument in less time than originally contracted for. Rental fees differ from instrument to instrument and in different areas of the country. Ask your child's music teacher or school about the fairness of price.

Do not buy a new or used instrument without having it looked at and played by someone who is an expert. He will be able to evaluate the pros and cons of a new versus an old instrument, the quality of the instrument's make and style, its condition, its tone-quality and the fairness of the price. This expert could be your child's teacher or some other professional who knows and plays the particular instrument. Teachers in the music department of your local school might be qualified to make such judgments, or would be able to recommend such a person to you.

Whoever is helping you pick out an instrument should be paid for his time and assistance. Even if your child's teacher helps you, it would certainly be proper to offer to pay for his time. This is well-spent money and can save you considerable grief in the long run. Sometimes a teacher will want to try several instruments of the same make and style before choosing the one that he considers best for his student. Just as no two Cadillacs drive and feel the same on the road, so no two clarinets of the same make and style will blow and feel the same way to an expert. We will go into more specifics about each instrument a little later.

It should be pointed out that with most instruments the "hot price" is usually just a starting point.

Many dealers offer to discount instruments so that "list price" is not often paid in full.

It is equally important to check on the reliability of the music store, dealer or private party from whom the purchase is being made. If it is a new instrument, be sure to inquire about the manufacturer's guarantee, and what free maintenance service is included. If it is a used instrument, it is important to have an agreement in writing from the music store or dealer about maintenance and repairs.

No matter how honest a music dealer is, he will naturally be anxious to sell you the instrument he has available or the one on which he makes the best profit. If you are purchasing a used instrument, in addition to having it tried out by an expert, it would also be wise to take it to an instrument repairman to get an estimate of what it would cost to put it in proper condition. Sometimes such repair work can cost almost as much as you are paying for the instrument. This is sensible only if the quality of the instrument is worth it, and your expert is the best judge of that.

As a general rule, most instruments do not improve with age. Usually your best bet is to buy a new one. The real exception to this rule is when the old instrument is a truly fine one, not a student model. Then it is sometimes worth paying for a necessary overhaul to put the instrument back into condition.

Follow these same rules even when purchasing a used instrument from your best friend. You may know someone who bought a brand-new flute for her son just last year. He doesn't want to play it any more, so now your friend is willing to sell it for less than its original price. If the instrument is a good make and style and is in good condition, this *might* be a very attractive buy. If the instrument is a poor quality student-model to start with and has been treated badly, it may be beyond repair (even though it may look beautiful). Your friend may not be aware of its deteriorated condition.

As we mentioned, a major cause of first-year dropouts in instrumental study is the discouragement and inconvenience of an instrument that needs frequent repair. The first way to cut down on repair work is to provide the child with a mechanically sound instrument.

Equally important is "preventive medicine." A child should begin his study by being taught exactly how to handle and care for his instrument. He will not then unwittingly damage it as he takes it out, holds it and puts it away. If the child complains that his instrument is not working properly, get it looked at right away, before the damage is increased and the child becomes discouraged. If the repair job is the direct result of improper handling, the parent must be sure that either the repairman or the teacher again explain to the student the correct handling of the instrument so there is not a repeat performance the next day.

How to Buy a Piano

Should you buy a used piano or a new one? Should you buy a grand piano or a vertical piano? Should you buy a piano with a full keyboard or is a smaller one just as good? How can you tell by looking at a piano if it is in good condition? What make piano should you buy?

Some pianos are considered the "brand names" in the field—among them are Steinway, Baldwin, Knabe, Sohmer, and Mason and Hamlin. The Bechstein, which is made in Germany, and the Yamaha, made in Japan, are both imported and each has its ardent admirers. But, as with automobiles, a lot depends on what you like, what you need, what you want to pay and what happens to be in the neighborhood. There are many good pianos that aren't mentioned above. And you may be unhappy with what would make someone else ecstatic. Well-made pianos that have been well taken care of do not deteriorate with age. Therefore it is a wise investment to buy a used grand piano that is even as much as thirty years old. The age of a piano can be determined by its serial number, which is on a metal plate inside the piano. This number can be checked with the manufacturer or with the piano technician brought in as a consultant. A used piano will cost dramatically less than a new one of the same size and make, and will often be of even finer quality than a new one. Used vertical pianos (old uprights, consoles or studios) are also a wise investment if they are in good condition, but they are much more difficult to find on the market than good used grand pianos. Console and studio upright pianos and grand pianos are superior to spinet pianos because their sounding board and strings are longer and therefore they produce a better tone-quality. Consoles and studio upright pianos are more in demand because they take up less space than a grand piano. (That is why good used ones are scarce.) There is no question that a grand piano will give the finest tone-quality. If you do not have a space problem, a grand might well be your choice. However, there is very little difference in string length and therefore in tone-quality between a 5-foot grand piano and a tall upright model of comparable quality. One must remember that part of the length of a grand piano is taken up by the keyboard. Be careful that you do not buy a used piano because of the looks of its case. A piano is a musical instrument, not a piece of furniture. Many people buy expensive spinets because they look so pretty in the living room. It is wiser to put the money into what is inside the case and end up with a musical instrument that will perform well for many years.

Grand pianos range in size from 5 feet to 9 feet in length. The 9-foot concert grand is rarely used any place but the concert stage or music studio. Most people prefer the smaller sizes for their homes. Modern vertical pianos range in height from about 40 to 46 inches, while a spinet is only 30 to 38 inches high. Old uprights are over 50 inches in height.

There are so many makes and sizes of pianos, and such a range of quality of used and rebuilt instruments, that expert advice is a must. Whether you buy a used piano from a close friend or through a private ad in a newspaper, at a public auction or from a reputable piano dealer or music store, do not make the purchase without bringing in your own specialist (a skilled piano repairman). Let him examine the instrument to see if it is mechanically sound and if the price is appropriate to the value. You will of course have to pay for this service, but it is well worth it.

The price range for pianos is broad: from $500 or $600 for a reconditioned upright to $28,000 for a new Steinway model D concert grand. A Steinway is one of the most expensive hand-crafted pianos on the market today. The company makes four different vertical or upright pianos, from 40 inches to 52 inches high. The least costly of these is about $4,700 new; the 52-inch-high model can be close to $8,000 with the most expensive case styling.

Steinway grands come in many sizes from the 5-feet 1-inch model S, to the model D concert grand of 8 feet 11¾ inches. The prices range from about $12,000 for the least expensive case style of a 5-foot 1-inch model, to about $28,000 for the concert grand.

Sohmer is another hand-crafted, American-made piano. This company specializes in vertical pianos and small grands, and their prices are far lower than Steinway's. Sohmer uprights range in height from 39½ inches to 45½ inches and cost about $2,500 to $3,500. They also make a 5-foot and a 5-foot 7-inch grand which are priced from about $8,500 to $9,600.

All piano manufacturers offer their grand pianos in a variety of case stylings. Ebony is the least expensive; an elaborate style, such as Louis XV, is among the most expensive.

The piano you choose depends on the space you have and the amount of money you wish to spend. Of course, if money is no object you can have a fine piano as well as a lovely piece of furniture. But buy with the former in mind, not the latter.

Regardless of the size or style of the piano you purchase, be sure it has a full keyboard of eighty-eight keys. Pianos with smaller keyboards (some of the top and some of the bottom notes have been eliminated) are manufactured but they are not recommended for use in the home for three reasons. First, the student does not develop the proper spatial sense at the keyboard. Second, the omission of these high and low strings greatly reduces the overtones that can be produced and decreases the quality of the instrument's tone. Third, it is impossible to play certain compositions.

Almost all pianos manufactured today have plastic keys rather than the traditional ivory ones. Some professionals swear the feel is the same; others refuse to play on them. But they have the advantage of not yellowing or chipping.

You can sometimes do better buying a used piano

from a individual or at an auction than through a piano dealer. Dealers in used instruments that were probably traded in for new ones or acquired at auctions usually put a good deal of money into refinishing the outside case to make the instrument look more desirable. Such refinishing is very costly. The inside of the piano is not always given such attention.

Although there is no written guarantee that goes with a piano you buy from a private party, there is almost always a guarantee with a used piano when it is purchased from a dealer or manufacturer. Sometimes a certain number of home tunings are included in the arrangement. Be sure that at least one home tuning is included because the piano will need it after being moved. On the subject of tunings, be sure it is specified that the piano will be tuned to "hold" at 440A. This refers to the number of vibrations per second (440) of the A above middle C, which is the tone that orchestral instruments and pianos usually tune to. If a piano has been out of use and untuned for a long time, it may take frequent tunings before it will come up to and remain at this pitch. If this is not specified in the written agreement, you may have to pay for the additional tunings.

There are some defects in used pianos which are relatively easy and inexpensive to repair and others that are more serious. Many people think that a crack in the sound board is very serious and sufficient reason for not buying the piano. A sound board can have many small cracks or even a big one and still produce a good tone. The important thing is that the structure of the sound board and the ribs is firm and secure. Your piano repairman will inspect the mechanisms of the action, the hammers, the felts, and he will check to see if the pins work well. If the pins do not hold, then the piano will not stay in tune and may require a whole repinning job.

Many piano dealers and manufacturers rent both new and used pianos, with an option to buy at the end of the rental period. They greatly increase their sales this way because they know that once the piano is in your home, you will most likely end up buying it.

Always check exactly what a rental fee or a purchase price includes, so you are not suddenly confronted with a lot of extras. Check to see if a piano bench or chair is included in the price. Also determine if the delivery and a tuning after the piano is in your home, are included.

How to Take Care of Your Piano

Some instruments are more prone to damage than others. It is almost impossible for a student to "break" a piano while practicing. The piano mechanism does go out of adjustment and will require repair from time to time, but it resists pretty rough treatment. Piano damage is more often the result of improper placement of the instrument, so that it is the victim of adverse temperature and humidity conditions. A piano should be placed where the heat and humidity are relatively constant: away from windows that may be open or that may let in the hot sun to bake the instrument; away from radiators with their direct heat and possibly steam as well. Do not place a piano in a draft or near an air-conditioning vent. Avoid dampness, and also extreme dryness. There are ways to dehumidify the inside of a piano if the room is unavoidably damp. Check this with your tuner.

The most usual damage to a piano is the result

of food or drink spilling into its mechanisms or of other foreign objects falling in. Don't allow small children to put their toys on the piano. Avoid taking off rings, bracelets or watches and resting them on the piano while you are playing. Such items can sometimes be very difficult to retrieve from the inside of the piano and they can damage the instrument if it is played before they are removed. Insist that no food or drink is brought anywhere near the piano. Give your child a snack before he sits down to do his practicing; at the risk of offending your guests, do not allow anyone to rest his cocktail glass on your piano. At the least, it may leave an ugly ring on the finish of the wood; if it should spill into the piano, it could ruin the felt and wood and metal that make up the mechanism. Do not put a vase of flowers with water on your piano. Even if the water does not spill and damage the instrument's case or insides, a vase or lamp will vibrate when the piano is played, causing a distracting noise.

Be sure to get your piano tuned, and have the key and pedal action checked by a competent person at least twice a year. Get a recommendation from your piano teacher or other very reliable source because good piano tuners and repairmen are scarce; you may have to make an appointment weeks in advance. A piano tuning costs between $35 and $40. Do not let even the most elementary beginner at the keyboard play on a badly out-of-tune instrument or one on which many keys stick or the sustaining pedal is out of adjustment. Such conditions add unnecessary burdens to the young musician.

It is inevitable that dirty fingers will find their way to the piano keyboard, particularly if you have young children around. Do not worry. Use only water on a damp cloth to wash the keys, but be sure the cloth is not wet enough to drip down into the keys. Treat the outside case of your piano as you would any piece of furniture. Guard it against scratches and water marks.

The best time to clean the inside of a piano is when the tuner is working on it. He generally dismantles the instrument to allow you to do a thorough job with a vacuum cleaner. But never attempt to do this by yourself. Often the tuner will do the job for you.

It's also a good idea to moth-proof the inside of your piano so the felts are not attacked. Do this only with solid cakes or blocks of camphor, never with a spray or with flakes. The camphor should not touch the strings, the moving mechanisms or the wood. Ask the piano tuner where the best position is in your piano to place the camphor and exactly how to do it.

If you have young children around, show them from the beginning how to respect the piano just as they are asked to respect the other fine furniture in your home. As long as all toys and crayons and other foreign objects are kept far away, there is little damage that can be done. Do not discourage a young child from experimenting with the sound of the new instrument; require that it be played only with the fingers.

How to Buy a String Instrument

Should you buy a new or a used string instrument? In student-quality instruments, it is usually better to buy a new one or at least one that is only a few years old and has been treated well.

What size instrument should you buy? When buying or renting a violin, viola, cello or double bass, first determine the correct size of instrument for the student. This is essential in the development of proper hand and body positions. The physical strain of playing on an instrument that is too large will often be enough to frustrate and discourage the student. Therefore, if the proper size is temporarily not available, it is better to have the student play an instrument that is a little too small rather than a little too large. The child's teacher should be consulted to determine the proper size. String instruments come full size or 4/4, 3/4 and 1/2 size. There are even some 1/4, 1/8 and 1/16 size violins. The correct size violin or viola is determined by a proper V shape at the elbow of the left arm when the player holds the instrument in correct playing position (first position).

The correct cello size is determined by the ability to play at the tip of the bow comfortably on all the strings without straining the right shoulder. The left hand must be able to comfortably reach a major third and also a whole step between the first and second fingers. The point where the neck of the cello connects with the body of the cello should come approximately to the player's chest bone, and the scroll should extend over the player's shoulder.

On the string bass, the left hand must be able to reach a major second from the first finger to the fourth finger. As with the cello, the player must be able to play comfortably at the tip of the bow on all four strings without straining.

The height of the cello and the string bass can be adjusted with the end pin. Therefore the most important measurements are left-hand span and right-arm length for bowing.

Be sure that the instrument comes with a sturdy, well-insulated carrying case. It should be well padded on the inside, have well-made latches so the case will not open accidentally, be equipped with a good carrying handle or strap and be either waterproof or water-resistant. If it is not, you can buy an inexpensive waterproof cover. The cello and string bass cases are usually made of waterproofed canvas or plastic. Be sure that they close securely with a zipper or with snaps. The bow must be the proper size for the instrument; its weight and resiliency are also important. Check to see if it is warped. There are fiberglass bows on the market which many teachers recommend for beginning students because they never warp and rarely break. The bow-screw should work easily so that the hair can be loosened and tightened correctly. Be sure the bow is well-haired.

All violins and violas must come equipped with a chinrest. If the instrument is equipped with steel strings, it should also have fine tuners. It is important that the bridge height is properly adjusted so the strings can be played easily. The tuning pegs must work smoothly and be able to hold in position. There is nothing more frustrating than an instrument that will not stay in tune.

In addition to a bow, an instrument and a case, a string player will need bow rosin, and it is a good idea to buy an extra set of strings.

A good student-quality carved violin or viola costs from $150 to $500, while a student-quality carved cello sells from $500 to $2,000. Any of these instruments, if made of plywood, will cost somewhat less, but will not produce as good a tone quality. One is likely to get the most reasonable price at a large music store of a major city where the volume of business is sizable.

Ordinarily, when buying a violin, viola or cello, a bow is not included in the price. A fiberglass violin or viola bow costs from about $20 to $35. A student-quality wooden violin or viola bow ranges from around $30 to $50. Fiberglass cello bows start at about $25 and student-quality wooden ones at about $50 or $60.

With all string instruments, it is essential that you consult an expert whom you trust when making a purchase. It is impossible for an inexperienced person to know the difference between a $150 violin and a $1500 one. As a matter of fact, the $150 instrument may "look prettier" to the inexperienced eye!

How to Take Care of Your String Instrument

The string instruments are considerably more fragile and breakable than the piano, but in terms of proper care, they have many things in common. The same rules concerning temperature and humidity conditions apply to all string instruments. Sudden changes in humidity and temperature can cause the wood to crack or the seams to open up. Most violinists and violists wrap their instrument in a soft cloth inside the case to give it added protection from dust, dirt and scratches. And be sure that the snaps or locks on the case work securely. A major cause of damage to instruments is a case that accidentally opens while it is being carried, causing the instrument to fall out. Also see that the student gets into the habit from the very start of keeping his instrument inside his securely closed case at all times when it is not being played. And be sure that the instrument is stored where it will not be knocked over accidentally or be within reach of small children in your family. Often an instrument is left, just for a few minutes, lying on a chair or a bed or on the floor, and someone will come along and sit on it or knock it over.

It is easier to find a safe storage place for a violin

or viola case than it is for a cello. Violins and violas are always in hard cases, but most student cellos come with either canvas or vinyl cases which do not protect them from being banged about. Therefore they must be stored so they will not fall or be knocked over. A corner of the room is usually a good place. There are hard-formed cello cases but they are quite expensive and are usually available only for full-size cellos.

There are some oil polishes, made specifically for string instruments, which are very good for cleaning and preserving the wood finishes. Do not use such polishes without consulting the teacher or repairman about the proper materials and the proper method.

We have suggested that you not discourage your small children from experimenting with the piano, so long as they learn immediately that it is to be treated with respect and may be played only with the fingers. This advice does *not* apply to the string instruments or any of the other orchestral instruments. They can be damaged very easily if not handled in the proper way. Therefore we will go one important step further and say that no friend or member of the family, no matter how careful he thinks he is, should ever be allowed to touch any orchestral instrument unless he is specifically instructed by someone who knows how.

If any damage is noticed on a string instrument, such as opened seams, or cracks or breaks, do not attempt to use the instrument until it is repaired or until a specialist assures you that it is safe to use it in that condition.

The hair on the bow should be loosened immediately after use. This will prevent the bow from warping. A student should never remove the hair from the bow; if the hair wears out it must be replaced by a skilled person. If the screw that tightens and loosens the hair on the bow does not work well, take the bow to a repairman.

The strings on the instrument should not be loosened after playing—they are always kept in tune. If the instrument is not going to be played for at least a few weeks, they should be slightly loosened.

Be sure the student washes his hands before playing his instrument. The fingerboard should be wiped clean of any dirt or hand moisture immediately after each use. Wipe the rosin dust off the body of the instrument. Use only a soft, clean cloth.

It is important that the bridge (the piece of wood that supports the strings and transmits vibrations to the body) is straight before the instrument is played because it is held in place only by the strings. The tension of the strings tends to pull it forward, and unless it is straightened, it may warp and eventually break. Sometimes, if the strings have not been kept taut by daily tunings at home, they will loosen to the point where they no longer hold the bridge in place. It is frightening for a beginning student to see a piece of his instrument fall off suddenly, if he has not been warned of the possibility. Unless it has been broken, its replacement is as simple as tightening the strings. This is why it is so important to provide the beginning student with a good instrument, one that will stay in tune relatively well (with good tuning pegs). It is terribly frustrating for a beginning student to find that his instrument is hopelessly out of tune every time he picks it up. It takes some time to become skilled enough to tune a string instrument. If the instrument is badly out of tune, practicing is almost impossible.

If your instrument does go out of tune frequently and the tuning pegs seem to be very loose, they can be made to grip more firmly by rubbing the peg well with ordinary white blackboard chalk. If the pegs are too tight and are hard to turn, they can sometimes be made to turn more easily by rubbing them with the slate of a pencil. If these two suggestions do not bring results, a repairman should be consulted.

It is most important to try to avoid the frustrations of minor mechanical mishaps at home. The student (and the student's parents, if he is very young) should seek some instruction at the very beginning about how to deal with the following basic repairs and adjustments. This will avoid constant phone calls to the teacher and unnecessary worries for the student.

1. Learn how to tune the strings. If you have a piano at home that is relatively well in tune, you can use it for the correct pitch. If not, you can buy an inexpensive pitch pipe.
2. Learn how to replace a broken string and always have extra strings on hand.
3. Learn how to adjust the bridge and line it up properly.
4. Learn how to tighten and loosen the bow the correct amount.
5. Learn the correct way to apply the rosin to the bow.
6. Learn exactly how to clean the instrument.

How to Buy a Clarinet

Should you buy a new or a used clarinet? Should you buy a wooden or a plastic clarinet? What size clarinet should you buy? What kind of mouthpiece should it have? What kind of reeds should you buy for the beginning clarinetist?

All clarinet students begin their study on the B-flat clarinet. It is the most important member of the clarinet family and it is very easy for a student to pick up the other clarinets once he has learned the basic techniques on the B-flat clarinet.

The best clarinets are made of wood. But student-quality instruments are also made of plastic. The list price of a good plastic, student-model clarinet such as the Bundy or the Evette, is about $300. However, in large music stores they are usually discounted by as much as 40 percent. The advantage of a plastic instrument for a beginner is that it won't crack. Naturally, the tone quality is not as good as it is with a wooden clarinet, but beginning students don't have enough tone control to make that a significant issue.

The list price of a fine professional clarinet such as a Buffet or a Selmer is about $1400. Here too, one can often get a substantial discount at a major store. If you are lucky enough to find a good used professional-quality clarinet and your expert tells you it is in good condition and priced fairly, you might consider buying it, rather than a new student-quality instrument. Buying a used student-quality instrument is risky unless it has obviously received very good treatment and the price is very reasonable. Even if money is no object, it is unwise to invest in a new professional-model clarinet for a beginning student. He will be just as successful on a good quality student-model or on a used professional one. Do not be frightened away from a used professional instrument just because there may be a small crack in its bore. If the crack is small and has been properly repaired, it will not in any way interfere with the proper functioning or tone of the instrument. If it is a large crack or if there are several cracks, chances are the instrument was not cared for very well, so it would not be a wise investment.

There are many things to look for in both new and used instruments, which is why it is essential to have an expert assist you. The important factors in choosing a clarinet are intonation, tone-quality, freedom of tone production and smooth functioning of the key mechanisms.

The choice of mouthpiece is perhaps more important than the clarinet itself. There are a variety of clarinet mouthpieces. Not only are they made of different materials but they are shaped differently. It is really not so important what the mouthpiece is made of (usually ebonite or crystal); the shape is what matters. The student should play on a free-blowing mouthpiece.

The thin piece of cane called a reed which fits on the mouthpiece and vibrates to produce the clarinet's sound is the smallest and the most important piece of equipment for the clarinetist. Reeds come in many sizes (thicknesses) and it is important for the student to have the proper size to suit his mouthpiece and his embouchure (mouth position). As a general guide, beginning students usually start on a number 1½ or number 2 reed and progress to a harder reed (thicker and therefore a higher number). Reeds cost very little (about 60¢) but they don't last very long. Be sure to buy a good supply at the start so that the student will not find himself without one when he is about to practice. Reeds come in boxes of twenty-five and it is cheaper to buy a full box than to buy them singly.

Instructions for caring for all the woodwinds begin on page 121.

How to Buy a Flute

Flutes used to be made only of wood, but now are made mostly of metal. Student-quality flutes are never made of wood, only some professional ones. Often a professional flutist who prefers a wooden flute will use a silver headpiece in order to produce a more brilliant tone. Wooden piccolos are very good because they produce a much more mellow tone than the metal ones. Student-quality flutes are usually made of nickel or nickel-silver. A closed-hole model is most often recommended for beginning students, and lists for about $300 to $350. Some good makes are Gemeinhardt, Armstrong, Bundy, Artley and Yamaha. As with clarinets, one frequently gets a substantial discount at a large store, sometimes as much as 40 percent off the list price, but more often 20 to 30 percent. French model open-hole instruments cost slightly more than closed-hole models.

Middle-of-the-line silver flutes like the Gemeinhardt model 3S or 3SB or the Armstrong model 80 list for about $900; they too can be purchased at a substantial discount in some stores.

Professional-quality flutes are usually made of silver but a few are made of gold and even platinum. Three outstanding makes are Haynes, Powell and Brannen-Cooper. Because these are hand-crafted instruments, there is a waiting period of four to ten years for a new one. Some teachers and music stores have standing orders with these companies for a few of the instruments each year. If you are fortunate and have contact with such a source, you may not have to wait too long. These fine flutes are not discounted and cost approximately $4,000. They do *not* depreciate in value. In fact, due to the long waiting period, used ones can be more expensive than new ones.

In recent years, several Japanese companies have started crafting flutes. They produce both professional instruments and advanced student models of high quality. Their professional models are slightly less expensive than the makes cited above, and they *are* discounted in the United States. Some of the Japanese makes are the Muramatsu, Sankyo Prima, Mirasawa and Yamaha.

Most flute teachers prefer to try out the specific instrument before the student buys it, since there are often variations in instruments, even those of the same make and style. Ease of blowing, tone-quality, intonation, and smooth functioning of the key mechanism are the important considerations when choosing a flute, just as they are for all woodwind instruments.

How to Buy an Oboe

All professional-model oboes are made of wood, but some good student-quality models are made of plastic. These plastic oboes, such as the Bundy, list for about $600 and can also be purchased at a discount. The advantage of a plastic instrument for a beginning student is that it will not crack and is usually guaranteed against breakage for a period of time. The intonation is quite good. The disadvantage is the difference in tone-quality, but this is really not a major factor for a beginner. Selmer makes a student-quality wooden oboe which lists for about $1,250.

One excellent professional oboe is the Laubin. It is made in New York and a new one costs about

$2,200. The waiting period for this custom-made instrument is about four or five years. The same company also makes an excellent student-model wooden oboe called the Barré. A new one is about $1,600. One of the finest professional instruments is the Lorée, made in France, which can be bought for approximately $2,500 new. It is hand-crafted and the waiting period is long.

The oboe uses a double reed and does not have a mouthpiece. Although almost all advanced students and all professionals make their own reeds, ready-made reeds can be bought in various strengths for beginning and intermediate students. These ready-made reeds are made of cane, and also of plastic. The plastic reeds, which don't have to be wet before playing, are very durable and do not respond to changes in weather. Cane reeds, of course, have a finer tone-quality if they are made very well, but they are extremely sensitive to temperature and humidity changes and rarely have the same playing quality two days in a row.

The mechanism of an oboe is extremely sensitive and the instrument should not be touched before proper care and handling have been learned from the teacher. It is essential that an expert help in the purchasing of an oboe. Be particularly careful when buying a used oboe because some old ones have antiquated fingering systems.

How to Buy a Bassoon

The bassoon is a large instrument made of wood or plastic and it uses a double reed just like the oboe's, only larger.

Student-quality plastic instruments such as the Bundy, list for about $1,300 and can be purchased at a discount. There are some very good middle-of-

the-line wooden bassoons such as King and Selmer, with a list price of approximately $2,000, but
also available at a discount. Fox makes a full line of
excellent bassoons, from student models through
fine professional models. They have a plastic student model for about $2,000 and their best profes-
sional model is approximately $7,500. All Fox in-
struments can be purchased at a discount.

The finest professional bassoon is the West
German-made Heckel, which costs about $10,000
new, and for which there is a waiting period of a
few years. If you are lucky enough to come upon a
good used Heckel, you might be able to purchase
it for as little as $5,000. An expert should always be
consulted when purchasing a bassoon.

The professional and the advanced student make
their own reeds of cane. But ready-made bassoon
reeds are available for beginning students.

How to Take Care of Your Woodwind Instrument

All the woodwind instruments have a delicate apparatus which can be easily damaged if not handled
correctly. Most repairs on a woodwind instrument
used by a beginning student (we are assuming the
instrument was in good working condition when it
was given to the student) are the result of improper
handling while putting the instrument together,
taking it apart, and cleaning it. A woodwind instrument is built in several pieces and the joints must
fit together accurately. A slight dent or bend in the
joint mechanism can cause the instrument to mal-
function.

The first and most important rule, therefore,
concerning the care and maintenance of all woodwind instruments is: Do not let the student take

the instrument out of its case until the teacher has given detailed instructions about how to do it properly. Be sure the student has taken the instrument out of the case, put it together, taken it apart, cleaned it thoroughly, and put it back in the case under the direct supervision of the teacher, before he is allowed to use the instrument alone at home. This care is not complicated or difficult and becomes a matter of routine after the first few weeks. But it is mandatory procedure if the instrument is to remain out of the repair shop for very long.

If anything does go wrong with any part of the mechanism, do not attempt to repair it yourself. It may be a minor thing that the teacher can fix in a minute with proper tools and know-how, or it may require the help of a skilled repairman.

Woodwind instruments need to be dried out thoroughly right after use, because wood absorbs moisture and will develop cracks if it is not kept dry. All the instruments in this family come equipped with a swab for that purpose. The oboe has a very delicate mechanism and it is equipped with a feather instead of a swab to clean its narrow bore. A special oil is available to coat the inside of woodwind instruments, but it must be used very sparingly or it will get into the pads and cause sticking. Check this with your teacher or repairman.

The joints of woodwind instruments are usually fitted together with corks. There is special cork grease which should be used to prevent them from drying out and to ease the job of putting the instrument together. If the corks are well greased, the student will not have to apply much pressure to fit the pieces together. But beware of putting on so much cork grease that the instrument slips apart while it is being played! Also, too much cork grease will find its way into the key mechanisms and cause sticking. When an instrument is brand new, it will require cork grease frequently, even as often as once a day. But after the first week or two, the joints will begin to go together easily. Eventually, grease can be applied once every few weeks. Metal flutes do not have cork; the metal joints fit smoothly together. They must be kept very clean and great caution must be exercised to avoid denting or bending them. Do not use cork grease on these metal joints. Use a mixture of ordinary rubbing alcohol and water (half and half) on a soft, clean cloth to clean them. The inside of a metal flute should be cleaned with a soft, dry cloth or hanky attached to the cleaning rod which comes with the instrument.

All the rules about temperature and humidity also apply to the woodwinds. Never expose a woodwind to extremes of temperature. If an instrument has been outdoors in very cold weather, allow it to warm up gradually before attempting to play it. The sudden contrast of warm air being blown into the cold bore of the instrument can cause cracks and checks (small cracks that do not go through the wood, appearing only on the surface).

If a woodwind instrument does go out of order, be sure to get it fixed immediately. Sometimes a very minor and inexpensive repair can make the difference between the student's being able to practice successfully or literally not being able to get a sound out of the instrument other than a squeak.

A woodwind instrument should not be left in one piece unless it is being used. If it is allowed to remain assembled for any period of time after its use, its joints may swell and "freeze" together. In any case, it must be taken apart after its use in order to clean it properly.

An instrument should always be handled with

clean hands. The keys may be wiped clean of per-spiration and dust with a soft dry cloth. Do *not* use silver polish on the keys, because the polish can get into the key mechanism. Woodwind instruments do well with a complete overhaul every few years; all the keys are removed, cleaned and polished, the wood is oiled, new pads and corks are put on, and the mechanism is thoroughly regulated. This complete and relatively expensive job is recommended only for a good instrument, not on an inexpensive student-model. If the job is done by an expert repairman, the result is a virtually new instrument.

Metal clarinets and saxophones follow the same general maintenance rules given for wooden instruments. But do not use bore oil on the inside of metal instruments. They should simply be wiped out with a swab or a clean dry cloth.

The most frequent and uncomplicated repair job on all woodwind instruments is the replacement of a pad. Some teachers may show their students how to replace pads on their instruments and may even suggest that they keep a set of extra pads and glue at home to use when necessary. Even if the teacher recommends that the instrument be taken back to the store to be fixed, it will only take a few minutes and will be very inexpensive. The pads last longer if the student keeps his instrument well cleaned after each playing, as moisture causes deterioration of the pads.

How to Buy a Brass Instrument

Brass instruments come in a wide range of models, from inexpensive student-quality instruments to the most expensive professional models. The major difference is in the quality of the mechanisms. Many teachers of brass instruments would prefer to have their students play on a good used professional-quality instrument as opposed to a new student-quality instrument for about the same price. Naturally, as with all instruments, it is important to have your child's teacher or other expert help you choose either a new or a used instrument. Student-quality trumpets such as the Bundy list for about $350 and can be purchased at a discount. A professional-quality trumpet such as Bach lists for about $700 to $800 and it too is discounted.

Trombone prices are about the same as trumpet prices; French horns, however, are more expensive. A student-quality French horn such as Bundy or King is about $900 but can be discounted to around $500 in a store with a large turnover. Professional-quality French horns such as King or Selmer can also be bought at a discount with a net price of $1,000 to $1,500. Most manufacturers produce a full line of each instrument, from inexpensive student-quality French horns to fine professional ones. It is important to seek an expert's advice about which model to purchase.

When buying a used brass instrument, corrosion on the inside is an important thing to look for. Dents can be more or less significant, depending on their size and location. A dent on the bell is not very important while a dent on the mouth pipe (or lead pipe) is critical in trumpets and in French horns. The slide is the most critical place for dents on a trombone. A tuba can have numerous small dents all over and not be affected.

There are many styles of mouthpieces for each of the brass instruments. The two variables are the diameter of the rim and the depth of the cup. The teacher is the only one to decide on the best mouthpiece for the beginning student.

When buying a brass instrument, either used or new, be sure it comes with a sturdy case to protect it from jars and bumps.

How to Take Care of Your Brass Instrument

The most important part of caring for brass instruments is keeping them clean. A player of a brass or any other wind instrument should not eat immediately before playing. If he does, small particles of food will inevitably find their way into the instrument. This promotes corrosion as well as interference with the working of valves.

Brass instruments should be given a "tub bath" at least once a year, or more frequently if food does get in. All parts of a brass instrument may be submerged and washed in lukewarm water and mild soap. The mouthpiece should be done frequently. When the entire instrument is given a tub bath, it should be completely taken apart first; all the valves are removed and washed separately; the slide of a trombone should be taken apart. The techniques of washing an instrument should be explained thoroughly by the teacher before the student attempts it on his own.

Valve oil should be applied to each valve every day before playing, about five or six drops per valve. Here, too, the specific technique should always be demonstrated by the teacher first.

If a valve sticks, it probably needs oil. If it sticks even after oiling, it probably needs to be removed and washed thoroughly. If it sticks after washing and oiling, then there may be something wrong with its mechanism and it should be checked by the teacher or a brass repairman.

If a brass instrument will not produce a sound

when blown, one of two things is probably wrong. First, the valves may have been replaced in the wrong order. The best way to avoid this is to remove only one valve at a time unless you are absolutely sure how to replace them in the correct order. Second, some foreign body—a pencil, some food, a toy, etc.—inside the instrument may be obstructing the flow of air.

In addition to keeping the brass instrument inside a sturdy case that was made specifically for it, remember not to put anything except the accessories inside the case. Most cases have a special compartment for the mouthpiece and valve oil. Students should not squeeze their music books or anything else inside the case with the instrument. It is very important to remember to remove the mouthpiece after each use. If it is left on it may become "frozen" to the lead pipe and perhaps will have to be taken to a repairman to be removed. Do not force it yourself if it does become stuck.

Be sure all brass instruments are kept away from young children who will not know how to handle them correctly and will damage them unintentionally. The slide of a trombone is very fragile; the slightest dent or bend can interfere with its proper functioning.

How to Buy a Guitar

You have probably heard that there are classical guitars and folk guitars, and that some guitars have steel strings while others have nylon strings. What should you buy?

Classical guitars are strung with nylon (formerly gut) strings. These guitars have a rather wide fingerboard, a round sound hole and a flat top. Folk guitars are strung with steel strings. The fingerboard is a little narrower than that of the classical guitar but it has the same flat top and round sound hole.

Classical guitars are usually plucked with bare fingers and the sound produced is rather delicate. Flamenco guitarists using this type of instrument can produce a more percussive tone by using their fingernails. Folk guitars with steel strings can be played either with the bare fingers or with a pick. Steel strings produce a much stronger tone than nylon strings.

Most professional American folk guitarists use steel strings. The classical or Flamenco guitar with nylon strings is easier for a young beginner.

The quality of a good instrument increases with age, just as it does with all string instruments. A poor-quality instrument will deteriorate, however. Its neck may have a tendency to warp and its bridge may begin to separate. Check to see if a neck is warped by placing a flat surface against it.

When shopping for a guitar, be certain the strings are strung close to the fingerboard (no higher than ⅛ inch). If they are higher, it will be very difficult to play.

As with all string instruments, it is impossible for an inexperienced person to know the difference between a $50 guitar and a $500 one. Indeed, the cheaper guitar might even "look prettier." Be sure to ask your child's teacher or another expert to assist you in the purchase.

A student-quality guitar with a carrying bag can cost from $50 to $150. Usually a guitar case is sold separately and must be fitted to the guitar. A reinforced cardboard case costs upwards of $25; a good padded wooden case can start at $50.

Do not look for a $20 or $25 bargain. Such a guitar will probably warp, crack or split. Cheap guitars that have been imported from such warm climates as Mexico, often react very poorly to change in climate. Beware of highly lacquered guitars with pictures stenciled on them.

All really fine classical guitars are hand-made in small quantities and therefore are more expensive than factory-made steel or nylon-string guitars.

How to Take Care of Your Guitar

The care of a guitar is similar to the care of any other string instrument. Keep it dry, and away from temperature extremes—sudden changes in humidity and temperature can cause cracks in the wood. When your guitar is not in use, it should be kept in a properly fitted case to protect it from scratches and bangs. Keep your guitar out of the reach of small children who may damage it accidentally. If the instrument is dropped on the floor, it can be severely damaged.

If you have a steel-string guitar, it is necessary to change the strings from time to time. Steel strings eventually "go dead" and also rust due to oxidation from finger perspiration.

Strings do break, so it is a good idea to have extra ones on hand. In addition to learning the proper way to tune the strings on a guitar, it is important for a student to know how to replace a broken string properly.

If your guitar does get damaged, do not try to repair it yourself. Take it to your teacher for advice or to a qualified guitar repairman.

How to Buy a Recorder

The recorder is perhaps the easiest of instruments to buy for a beginning student. If you are equipped with the following information, you can safely make the purchase without the help of an expert. However, if you are purchasing a recorder for an advanced student, it would be wise to get expert advice about makes, sizes and discount prices.

There are six sizes of recorders which are listed in order of size, from the smallest (the highest in pitch) to the largest (the lowest in pitch): sopranino, soprano, alto, tenor, bass and great bass. Young beginners should start on a soprano recorder; it can be handled comfortably by small fingers and has a vast beginning literature. Older children or adults can comfortably begin on an alto or even a tenor recorder. These three sizes are the most used of the recorder family and are the only ones that should be considered for purchase by the beginner. Don't be confused by the German and English names for these sizes. Soprano recorders are also called descant or sopran recorders; alto recorders are called treble or alt recorders. Tenor recorders have the same name in Germany and England as in the United States.

If you are buying a soprano recorder for a child to use in his school music program, you have two decisions to make. Should you buy a wooden or a plastic recorder? Should you buy a recorder that has German or English (baroque) fingering?

There are advantages to buying a plastic instrument for a young student. First, it is less expensive than a wooden one. Second, the plastic instrument will not crack because of moisture left in the instrument; nor will it be sensitive to temperature and humidity conditions or have to be handled with the same care as a wooden instrument. The argument against plastic recorders used to be that their tone-quality and intonation were inferior to wooden recorders. For student-quality instruments, this is

The soprano and alto recorders are the two best sizes for young students. Here they are being played side by side, with the larger one, the alto, on the left.

really no longer true. There are some excellent plastic instruments on the market today with very good intonation and a tone-quality that will remain constant. A wooden recorder will react to moisture and temperature and will not retain its good tone-quality if it is not cared for properly. If the child loses a plastic recorder, the parent is not horrified at the thought of replacing it as the financial investment is minimal. A student-quality plastic soprano recorder lists for about $4 to $8 and can usually be purchased at a discount. One of the best soprano recorders is the Japanese-made Aulos.

If you are buying a recorder for a more advanced child or for an adult beginner, it would be preferable to invest in a better quality wooden instrument. Two excellent makes are Kung, manufactured in Switzerland, and Moeck, manufactured in Germany. Various woods are used in the manufacture of recorders. These include maple, rose and pear woods. The list price of these fine instruments starts at about $45 and goes considerably higher. Like plastic recorders, they can often be found at a discount.

Be sure your recorder comes with a case and a cleaning swab.

Recorders are made with two different fingering systems, German and English (baroque). The two instruments look alike and have the same fingerings with the exception of a few notes, but for a young beginner, the German fingering is much easier and is therefore strongly recommended over the baroque. Intonation problems with the former, however, make it necessary for the advanced player to switch to a baroque fingering instrument later. An adult or older child beginner should therefore start out on the baroque fingering and avoid having to switch later. The reason the German fingering is recommended for young students in a school situation is that it is easier and that most of the students will not go on to be advanced recorder players but will more likely move on to one of the orchestral instruments. In most cases, therefore, the switch from German to baroque fingering will not have to take place.

It is very easy for a recorder player to switch from one size recorder to another because the fingerings of the different instruments are almost identical.

If you are planning to buy a good wooden recorder, it is advisable to consult an expert. Wooden recorders vary in tone-quality and intonation from one instrument of the same make to another, just as with all other woodwind instruments. These are delicate instruments and must be treated with care, particularly when they are new and are being "broken in."

How to Take Care of Your Recorder

Plastic recorders are very simple to take care of. They should be kept clean. They come equipped with a swab and should be taken apart (in two or three pieces depending on the make) and swabbed after each playing. Recorders roll very easily and should not be placed on top of a table where they may roll off and break or crack.

A wooden recorder must be treated with the same respect and care as any other delicate woodwind instrument. The most important factor is keeping it clean and dry. As soon as you have finished playing a recorder, it must be thoroughly swabbed out to remove the moisture. When playing the recorder, try to keep your mouth and lips as dry as possible. If moisture is allowed to remain inside the recorder, it will cause the wood to swell and crack. Be very careful when using the swab that you do not damage the delicate structure inside the mouthpiece. There is special woodwind bore oil that can be applied to the inside of a wooden recorder to help protect it from moisture. Apply this very sparingly and do not oil the inside of the mouthpiece. Be sure the recorder is thoroughly dry of saliva before applying this oil and then allow at least a day for it to be absorbed before playing the recorder again. A new recorder should not be played more than a few minutes at a time. A short break-in period is necessary for the conditioning of the wood.

Recorders, like all woodwind instruments, are sensitive to extremes of temperatures and humidity. If you carry a recorder outside on a cold day, do not play it immediately after bringing it indoors. Let it adjust to the temperature change gradually.

Otherwise, the warm air that you suddenly blow into the cold instrument can cause the wood to crack.

If the recorder has cork on its joints, lubricate the cork with cork grease that is made for that purpose and which can be purchased in any musical instrument store. If your recorder has waxed thread on its joints, they sometimes become too loose. You can fix this by adding a little more thread on top of what is already there—plain sewing thread or dental floss is fine for this purpose. Keep the recorder inside its case when not in use. Keep it out of the reach of small children and in a place where it is not likely to fall or be knocked onto the floor.

6

Your School and Community Music Programs

The school music class has often been referred to as the "music appreciation" class. This is a most unfortunate label and has been the butt of school-yard jokes for decades. Indeed it has often been a classroom where music is depreciated. We would not think of calling math or history class math appreciation or history appreciation. This simply does not describe the activities which should be taking place in such a class at any grade level.

A comprehensive, well-integrated music curriculum in elementary, junior and senior high school provides its students with as broad a musical experience as possible. One can participate on three levels: Creation; Interpretation; Appreciation.

Music is a performing art which cannot be properly understood and used unless the skills of the language are learned. So any good music program must first stress these basic elements of the language of music and its written notation. The student should have an opportunity to *make* music, not merely to like it. People enjoy and "appreciate" much more when they understand something, and when they can do it themselves, even on a primitive level. Music appreciation does not make up a music curriculum any more than listening to records of people speaking French constitutes a course in French. The greatest joy is in the doing; the next greatest joy is in listening with understanding.

The music class which meets anywhere from one to five times per week can provide students from elementary through senior high school with this comprehensive experience. The music curriculum should provide a thorough analytical listening program, including some courses in ear training, theory analysis and sight-singing. It should provide students with an opportunity to hear and identify musical forms, modes, period styles and become generally aware of the relationship of music to society. But it should pay the greatest attention to the more creative aspects. This can be done not only by playing the music of others and interpreting music, but by giving each student an ample opportunity to create his own sounds. As we give each of our children, from kindergarten on, a chance to put paint on paper, to mold with clay and to draw with crayon, so each child should have a chance to create sounds and to express his sense of the rhythm and pulse of life through music of his own making. A good beginning can be made with the child's own instrument, his voice.

Singing is an essential part of any music program. Young children sing as they play—they make up melodies and songs freely, often without realizing they are "composing." This creative and spontaneous use of the voice is found in virtually every young child in virtually every culture. This is one of the beautiful qualities of life, and it will be carried into adulthood if it is not stifled in the classroom or at home. Specific information about the voice and vocal training can be found in Chapter 3. Let us assume here that singing should be part of the overall music experience.

Creative singing, rote singing (unison and in parts) and singing from notation are all essential elements of a classroom music program. Because the voice is everyone's first musical instrument, it should be cultivated and trained from infancy on. Whether it is singing simple folk melodies or learning the intricacies of a motet, whether it is country music or a Handel oratorio, people have the urge to sing. If you have ever heard a group of young voices singing for pure pleasure, you know how beautiful all children can sound.

Other instrumental training should also begin at the earliest stages. Children are fascinated by making sounds and by listening to them. All sorts of melodic and percussive instruments can be used successfully by very young children. By the time a child is in the second grade or so, he is probably ready for a simple melody instrument, such as the song flute, flutophone or tonette. These are plastic, cost about $2, and are excellent beginning instruments for the young child.

Some people ask: "Why not start the child on the recorder and not bother with a 'toy' instrument that is inferior in tone and smaller in range?" There are some good reasons. These simplified recorders are much easier to play for the younger child who still may have some difficulty with small motor coordination of his fingers. The tone can be controlled more easily too, so the young child is almost guaranteed a successful and exciting first instrumental experience with relatively little effort.

Some other parents ask "Why not wait a year or two longer and then start the child on the recorder as his first experience?" There are three good reasons for starting out as early as is practical with the tonette-type instrument. First, this preparation and training is transferable to the recorder; only a very few notes are fingered differently. Second, a child who has had tonette experience will progress much more rapidly on the recorder and will find it less frustrating and more satisfying. The beginning recorder student who lacks this training may not progress as quickly. Third, anything which adds another dimension to a child's musical experience and pleasure at an early age is desirable.

What about the place of the recorder in the school music program? The song flute prepares the child for the recorder just as the recorder prepares the child for all forms of instrumental study which may follow. In addition, the recorder is a very satisfying end in itself for the student who does not wish to study an orchestral instrument. There is a large recorder literature and much opportunity for ensemble playing on all levels.

The student who has had some pre-instrumental training on song flute or recorder usually embarks on the study of an orchestral instrument with many advantages. He knows how to read music melodically and rhythmically and he has experienced the disciplines and rewards of instrumental ensemble playing. Now he can face the challenge of applying what he knows to the study of another instrument.

Group Instrumental Instruction

Some school systems offer free group instruction in band and orchestral instruments beginning in the fourth or fifth grade. Your child should take advantage of this good opportunity. There are social and emotional values to be gained along with the musical values of such an experience.

For a modest financial outlay (usually just the rental of an instrument and the purchase of a method book), your child can have the chance to try an instrument and begin a new and exciting experience in music-making. You may ask: "Why should I arrange for him to take group lessons in school when he is likely to make faster progress if I arrange private lessons for him outside of school?" In the early stages of instrumental study, a child does not necessarily progress faster in a private lesson. If the teacher is skillful, the child is helped by the built-in motivation of healthy group competition and by the excitement of ensemble playing. By starting out in school with a teacher who is trained in all the instruments, the child can more easily be switched from one instrument to another if the first choice does not work out well.

The school instrumental music teacher is one of the most qualified people to judge which instrument your child is best suited for. Not only does she know your child musically, but she also knows him academically and socially.

The social and emotional values of group lessons can often be dramatic. Here a child can "belong" and be successful in school even if he has not been successful in other academic areas. Music can provide a chance for an emotional outlet and a social contact that can be a boost to a child's total development. The opportunity to be a needed and important member of a band or orchestra can do a great deal for the emotional health of a youngster who has not yet found his way.

After a year or two of group instruction, it is usually wise for a student to receive private instruction in order to make the most progress on his instrument. By then he has most likely settled on an instrument which he likes and one on which he can be expected to make reasonable progress. He will then be ready for the more intensive instruction which a specialist can be expected to provide in a private lesson.

After a child has begun private instruction, the school program should continue to provide him with opportunities for ensemble rehearsal and performance in school orchestras, chamber music groups, a concert band, perhaps a marching band and jazz and pop groups as well. Let us take a look at these activities and evaluate their worth in a school setting.

The symphonic band is made up of woodwind, brass and percussion instruments. The only string instrument is the bass violin, and it is not always present. This type of band uses its instrumental sections to parallel a symphony orchestra. The clarinet section plays the role that the violin section does in an orchestra. The first clarinetist is the concertmaster of a band just as the first violin player is the concertmaster of a symphony orchestra. There is a great deal of music written for symphonic band and it is exciting to be a member of such a group.

The marching band is usually made up of the same students who perform in the symphonic band. It performs at football games and other athletic events and parades in the community on various holidays. The musical value of this group is somewhat limited, but its social value can be great.

Rehearsing for a weekly show at the football game is perhaps a healthier way of spending the late afternoons than just "hanging around." It can be an acceptable outlet for a great deal of pent-up energy. The less athletically inclined have a sense of pride and belonging, and the somewhat shy and less outgoing student is where the action is. It gives virtually everyone a chance to participate actively as a member of a group. In addition to all the obvious educational values that the band can have, it is also fun for practically everyone who joins.

When the football season ends in the late fall, many of the same students are then ready to settle down to the rehearsing and performing of more "serious" music in the symphonic band.

The school orchestra   is made up of all the bowed string instrument players and many of the woodwind, brass and percussion players. There is a vast literature written for this group. When they become advanced enough, they can perform the works of the symphonic orchestra repertoire. The musical values of playing with such a group cannot be overstated.

It is much more difficult to have a first-rate school orchestra than it is to have a fine school band, because so much depends on the stringed instruments, which are more complicated to learn than the wind instruments during the first years of study. Because the marching band can often play an important role in school-community relations, some school systems put a greater emphasis on their bands than on their orchestras. This is unfortunate for the latter. We could use more first-rate school orchestras.

The chamber music group can provide the most sophisticated and exciting music-making experience for any musician, young or old, experienced or novice. Chamber music refers to a small group of musicians (two or more) performing together without a conductor. This type of performance includes duets, trios, quartets, quintets, sextets, etc., in various combinations of strings, woodwinds, brasses, voices, piano or percussion instruments. A good school music program should provide opportunities for its more advanced musicians to get together in such groups and be coached in the art of chamber playing. This is the kind of playing that is most readily available to adults. It can provide endless hours of pleasure throughout a person's lifetime.

One excellent way for adults and advanced students to make contact with other instrumentalists in their area who might be interested in playing chamber music, is to join the organization, Amateur Chamber Music Players. Their address is Box 547, Vienna, Virginia, 22180, and their phone number is (703) 281–1238. This service organization links chamber music players across the country—advanced students and professionals alike. It publishes a listing of its members according to location, instrument, experience and ability. Each member is asked to complete a rating form which establishes his or her experience and ability.

Vocal groups are often the backbone of the school music performing program. The voice is the one musical instrument we all have, and we should all have a chance to enjoy it. Glee clubs and school choruses should exist on virtually all grade levels. There should always be some vocal group open to students with no special training, in addition to groups for the more advanced vocal students. These can be madrigal groups, small chamber singing groups and choirs.

Jazz and rock groups represent the music of the young people themselves. They are often far more capable of expressing it and feeling it than the music teachers around them. A time and place should be set aside to give these groups a chance to rehearse and to perform for school and extracurricular functions. By not excluding the students who prefer this type of performing, the school may be able to persuade them to join some of the other groups and thus broaden their musical horizons.

The school summer music program varies from one community to another. In a school system with a well-developed and active music program, summer music can be quite important. There are often group instrumental music lessons offered, just as during the school term. There may also be daily band and orchestra rehearsals and frequent concerts given, some of them perhaps outdoors. Such a summer music program is ideal for many youngsters who do not have a chance to go to camp or to travel. It is a fine way for a young musician to "keep in shape" on an instrument and it is also a good social opportunity for youngsters who otherwise find it difficult to make new friends easily.

Sometimes a community will sponsor a music festival or have guest artists or teachers in the community for the summer. That can often provide a bit of excitement and a chance to get a new point of view and perhaps participate in a memorable concert. The inspiration provided by a visiting teacher or performer can be an important spur for the development of a young musician.

Adult performing groups play an important role in most communities. These are groups which are usually formed by the local music teachers and sometimes some very fine amateur players. They often welcome some of the more mature and advanced student players. They can be as good as the local talent permits, and the quality in some communities is high indeed. If a town is fortunate enough to have a fine conductor who is willing to organize a symphony orchestra, band or chorus, and the community has enough talent to make up a first-rate group, the results can be exciting for all concerned. Even in a large city such as New York, where a true "community sense" is rare, there are frequently fine amateur performing groups, both vocal and instrumental. This sort of thing can offer an excellent performing opportunity for a serious young player. For those who are thinking of preparing for a career in music (see Chapter 7), these are excellent training grounds. For the good amateur or advanced player, they can be a source of great pleasure. The local artists can give a community a sense of pride, perform for fund-raising projects and often act as hosts when a professional artist or group makes a local appearance.

Church and temple choirs offer additional opportunity for musical participation and performance. Indeed choirs have been a traditional starting point for many fine professional singers. The choirmaster is often an excellent music teacher and coach, and frequently includes instrumentalists in performances at special times of the year. The church is also a place where young pianists can gain their first exposure to the organ.

It may come as a surprise to some readers to learn that each year more Americans pay to hear concerts than pay to watch baseball games. We are a nation of music lovers and one thing it will take to keep us that way is enough chance for young players to find the joys of performing in the community.

Methods of Instruction

There are many different methods of instruction used in the music classroom today. Some are old; some are new. The specific method used is not nearly as important as the skill of the teacher in presenting the method. Some teachers manage to combine the principles of several methods in their classes. This flexibility is usually good because it allows the teacher to use his own skills to their best advantage and allows instruction to be geared to the specific needs of that teaching situation and to the differences among individual students.

Try not to be impressed or overwhelmed by the names of new methods. Find out first how the new approach fits in to the total program and what it specifically offers the student. Here are descriptions of some of the better-known and more successful methods which have been developed and practiced over the years. Although they contain similar elements, and are basically sound in their approach, they differ with respect to their goals.

The Dalcroze method. This well-known method approaches all the elements of music (rhythm, tempo, melody, harmony, dynamics, phrasing, form, etc.) through the use of the body, with ample opportunity at all stages for creative expression. Dalcroze Eurythmics use the body and rhythm instruments to explore the elements of rhythmic expression and form. Many teachers who are not specifically trained in the Dalcroze method use some of its ideas because of its longstanding success and popularity. In a Dalcroze Eurythmics class the children dramatize freely with their bodies and respond to the improvised music played by the teacher. Everyone is personally involved with the music and participates physically. They experience a scale, for example, by stepping off the tones of the scale across the floor, moving step by step. They learn to "walk" melodic dictation, taking single steps when the melody moves stepwise and jumping the proper distance when the melody line makes a jump. They often develop a keen inner sense of rhythm, melody and form long before they intellectually grasp how "advanced" they really are!

The Dalcroze method was developed by Emile Jaques-Dalcroze, a Swiss composer and educator (1865–1950). He developed his system of eurythmics while teaching at the Geneva Conservatory from 1892 to 1909. The Institut Jaques-Dalcroze was opened in Geneva in 1915. Some of his students and followers, notably Miss Hilda Shuster, brought his teachings to the United States. The Dalcroze School in New York City offers not only a wide variety of courses of instruction for adults and youngsters but a comprehensive course in the Dalcroze system for those teachers who wish to learn it first-hand. Many graduates have gone on to apply its methods in different teaching situations in widely scattered localities.

The Orff system, or the Orff-Schulwerke method, is another special system that has a number of adherents in the United States. The method was originated by the composer and teacher Carl Orff (1895–1982), who developed special Orff instruments which have become part of the method. These instruments include both melodic and fixed pitch percussion devices. The method itself builds on the natural rhythmic responses found in virtually all children and provides them with opportunities for creative improvisation and ensemble experience.

Orff instruments are manufactured in Germany but are readily available in the United States. With a full set of these instruments, including gongs, bells, cymbals and drums, and a well-trained teacher, young children can get a very good musical start with this method.

The Kodály method was developed by the Hungarian composer and educator, Zoltán Kodály (1882–1967). He brought together ideas presented by Orff and Dalcroze, among others, and added his own elements. His approach emphasizes a thorough, graduated system of music education beginning in nursery school. Kodály also emphasized the use of the voice and developed play songs, chants and games to aid in teaching rhythm, meter, accents and so on. In addition, Kodály pioneered in the use of a system of hand signals. Each signal is a visual representation of one note of the diatonic scale. These hand signals are used to reinforce what the children hear and help them to write what they hear and see as well. A creative teacher skilled in the use of this method can provide an excellent start for a young music student.

The Suzuki method, a recent innovation in string instruction, has caught the public's fancy. It has certainly produced some spectacular results. This system was developed and promoted after the Second World War by a Japanese teacher, Shinichi Suzuki. He theorized that even though the violin is one of the more demanding instruments, instruction on it should not be delayed until the fourth grade. He started youngsters on small-sized violins almost as soon as they were able to hold the instrument and bow. He also felt that it was important to learn to play by ear right away, and leave the struggle with both technique and note reading until later. That struggle, Suzuki felt, was often so discouraging that young players would drop out quickly rather than endure the long months of frustration. And so, he taught three-, four- and five-year-olds by asking them to imitate. The first songs are memorized without any notes being learned. Before you know it, a six-year-old with no previous exposure to the instrument is learning to play a simple melody.

Before the first formal lesson, the Suzuki student hears a record or another person playing simple tunes on the violin. He gets used to the sounds, the melody, the way the musical line moves. Young children are able to memorize very quickly—after a few repetitions, the tune is in their heads.

The next step in the Suzuki method is to invite the child to a group lesson just to observe and receive his first instrument. This will be a violin proportioned to the child's size. Even the smallest child can begin, for there are violins which are one-sixteenth size.

With this system, the parent, usually the mother, becomes an active partner. She goes to each lesson and adds constant encouragement and attention as the young violinist goes about memorizing the first simple tunes. At no point in these beginning stages is there any learning of notes; rather, it is a rote method of obtaining quick success and satisfaction with simple materials. The theory is that the child, experiencing the thrill of success, will be more ready to persevere when the difficult steps are taken later—and this is, of course, the way that children learn a language.

Fingering and bowing techniques and proper position are taught, all before notes are discussed. When enough pieces are memorized, and the students have acquired a good bit of technical proficiency, the notes of those pieces are then used to teach note reading.

Perhaps there is no more startling sight and sound in music education than a diminutive Suzuki student confidently playing a demanding sonata or concerto. Demonstrations of the method by its originator, accompanied by some of his most gifted pupils, have caused quite a sensation among music educators and interested parents in the United States in the past few years. There are now hundreds of school systems using the Suzuki method. It is also having a strong effect in Japan, where many capable young violinists are being trained. They are beginning to populate the major orchestras of the world, and are helping to establish a new tradition of violinists. This is an important new source of talent for an instrument whose top virtuosi were becoming less numerous.

The success of the Suzuki method has helped indicate something that most music educators today seem to agree upon. Instrumental instruction has, in the past, proceeded too much from notation in the beginning stages and not enough by ear. There is reason to believe that the success of Suzuki will cause a swing toward teaching young players to rely on their ears. The human ear is a fine piece of natural equipment and the young musician who learns to use it early is usually far ahead as he develops his instrumental technique.

The enthusiastic participation of parents in the Suzuki method has shown that they can be effective partners in their children's music education if there are specific goals. The role of the parent needs to be clearly spelled out by the teacher and then respected by both parent and child.

There are many other teaching methods in use. There are special books which claim that learning to read notes and learning to play an instrument are some sort of game. Some of these methods use little poems and various mnemonic devices; others attempt to teach notes and chords by using colors. Most of these are borderline methods at best. They generally waste time and do no special harm—but the time-wasting itself can discourage a bright child from further participation.

Watch out for anything promising spectacular results overnight or claiming that the best way to learn music is to learn something else first!

The happiest situation is an enthusiastic teacher who believes in what he or she is doing and really knows how to use whatever method is chosen. This gives the child the best chance in the world. Even the finest method will not be effective if the teacher is weak or doesn't believe in it. If you have found a good teacher, then follow her method, even if it isn't the one you have heard so much about, or the one with which your neighbor's child is doing so well.

7

Careers in Music

There are many career opportunities in music for those with talent and persistence. The purely artistic careers involve performing, composing, arranging, teaching and related activities. Music production covers a broad spectrum from producing concerts or engineering recording sessions to a variety of other "backstage" functions.

Arts administration is a relatively new and growing field. It is an area for those with both a love for and a knowledge of music and related arts, who wish to be involved in management. Despite the withdrawal of some government support for the arts in recent years, there has been a gratifying growth in the number of performing groups throughout the United States. These groups need competent professionals to manage their financial and artistic growth and development. So it is not surprising that this need is now being filled by a new breed of young managers. Often possessing a graduate degree, they are taking over the leadership of arts organizations.

Several universities have recognized this need and have created graduate programs for the training of arts administrators. Among these is Columbia University in New York City, where Schuyler Chapin, former General Manager of the Metropolitan Opera, has played a major role in developing this program.

There are several organizations which help to sponsor, train and place arts administrators. For a number of years, the National Endowment For The Arts, with headquarters in Washington, D.C., has offered a fellowship program to a select group for on-the-job training. The major concert orchestras of America have banded together and their organization, the American Symphony Orchestra League (ASOL), located at Box 669, Vienna, Virginia, 22180, also offers a program designed to develop and train professional orchestra managers. Another organization, Theatre Communications Group Inc., at 355 Lexington Avenue, New York, N.Y. 10017, publishes a bi-weekly bulletin called "Artsearch." This is a nationwide employment service bulletin for the performing arts, listing job openings in all areas of the arts.

Another useful source of job information is Opportunity Resources For The Arts, Inc., at 1501 Broadway, New York, N.Y. 10036. This non-profit organization serves as a resource bank of candidates for positions in the arts. It is called upon by arts organizations to present qualified candidates for open positions.

The field of arts administration is one that should continue to grow even as the arts experience difficulty procuring adequate funding.

There are a number of other career and job opportunities in the music business. While training as a musician is not an absolute necessity, a solid musical background is often a great help. Such careers might include owning and operating a music store or manufacturing and repairing instruments and audio equipment. There is also the interesting position of A&R representative (Artists & Repertoire) which involves choosing the material and artists for the multiple records and tapes produced each year.

Performing. Perhaps no other field in our society is subject to as few rules as the performing career. But one thing is almost certain: conspicuous success is only for a handful, those chosen few who possess a virtually unique combination of three factors. These are great talent, great ambition and drive, and great good fortune. At any one point in time there are very few "great" violinists or pianists or singers. The top-notch performers are unquestionably the exceptional people. There is a vast gulf between these truly outstanding performers and the large numbers of first-rate professionals who rank just below them.

An eminent conductor, talking backstage just before a major concert, said, "We are going to give four performances of this work. We must bring to bear absolute, total concentration. We must try in each performance to reach the heights. But, of course, I know that the four performances will not be equal. The very best, the finest professional musicians will achieve a beautiful and fully realized performance in two out of the four. But the truly great performer will do it in three out of four! Let us see if we cannot achieve that!"

If you have ever known any great artists, or read about them, you will know how rare they are and what incredible dedication, concentration and singleness of purpose they have. Only with enormous sacrifice, almost inhuman abilities, the good fortune of being in the right place at the right time, having the right teacher, and having that natural ability to communicate an art to an audience in some intangible, almost magical way, is a person likely to achieve true greatness as a performer.

Just below these exalted few, however, is an extensive group of performers, often brilliant and frequently of international renown, who make up the body of working musicians in the world. Within that group there is a wide range of abilities and earning capacities. Though there are many types of performing opportunities, this can be a difficult and demanding career. First, there is the instrumentalist or vocalist who is successful in developing a career as a soloist. Such a person must have great dedication and devotion and must be willing to make various sacrifices for his art. Often, a person's personal and social life takes a very secondary place in this scheme of things. He must also be far superior to his colleagues in technique, musicianship and general presence. This group would include many of the performers just a shade below a Horowitz or a Galway, a Bernstein or a Domingo.

Then there is the larger group of players who are good enough to command jobs with the major symphony orchestras of the world, and the vocalists who can sing the supporting roles in major opera companies. In short, those musicians who are so skilled they are virtually assured of steady employment with a major performing group.

These people have the advantage of holding relatively secure, permanent positions. They are usually protected by strong unions, insuring them of a year-round income which they often supplement with recording work and teaching. Some of the disadvantages of such work are having to play music chosen by others with many of the same works repeated over and over, long and difficult touring schedules, and a lack of opportunity to be more than one of many instrumentalists in a large section. Some orchestral musicians have found the routine stultifying after a period of time, but are reluctant to give it up because of the guaranteed income which is notoriously absent for most people in the field.

While many orchestra players can earn a good

living, especially the first desk players (the section leaders for each instrumental group) and those who do occasional solo work, this is not a field for those who dream of large incomes. The orchestral musician in the United States today will earn between $10,000 to $40,000 a year, depending on the quality, location of the orchestra, and the length of the season. The country's major orchestras all have year-round seasons, good recording contracts and well-sponsored tours. Some smaller cities have short seasons, in which case, an orchestra musician does not really have a full-time occupation. But for those able to make the grade with a large and stable orchestra, excellent fringe benefits and pensions are now the rule. For many people, it is a good, rewarding career and a very satisfying way of life. Age, sex and race no longer seem to be significant barriers.

The New York Philharmonic, Boston Symphony, Cleveland Symphony, Los Angeles Philharmonic, Philadelphia Symphony and Chicago Symphony are regarded as perhaps the best, though one will get an argument in such places as Houston, Pittsburgh and St. Louis! There are changes all the time, but New York, Cleveland, Boston and Philadelphia have the longest tradition of remaining very close to the top rank of world orchestras. There are also many "second-rank" orchestras which serve as excellent training grounds for just-turned-professional younger musicians. Many of these orchestras have a twenty-to-thirty-week season and some go on tours; they have been the first orchestras for many of today's best orchestral players. A group such as the Buffalo Philharmonic has not only spawned orchestral players but also provided the late William Steinberg with a post as music director before he went on to Pittsburgh and Boston. In recent years, the American composer and conductor, Lukas Foss, and the young maestro, Michael Tilson-Thomas, served as music directors for the Buffalo Philharmonic.

Young players do have a chance for orchestral jobs. Mixed in among some of the more venerable players you will find more and more young American-born and trained players. However, a very gifted young performer will almost always attempt a solo career first, before considering the orchestral audition.

When orchestras have openings, they usually announce the fact in one or more of the music trade papers. Anyone interested should have ample experience and be prepared for some competitive auditioning, particularly for the coveted first desks, the section leaders. The top spot is that of concertmaster, a job held by the first desk player of the first violin section. Often this player is the most experienced leader, someone who is frequently a conductor in his own right.

There is yet another world made up of the fine musicians who play in the orchestras and bands that perform pop music. They play in theater orchestras, are hired for much of the commercial recording that is done, play background music for television and films, and play in clubs and as entertainers for a variety of public and private gatherings.

These musicians are members of the American Federation of Musicians. As such, they will rehearse and perform only for union-scale rates. Some of the players belong to groups which perform more or less regularly during a season; a season can last only a few weeks or be virtually year-round. But for the many performing jobs that are "one shots" or single performances, there is usually a union contractor who calls upon the local musicians on his list as he receives requests for performers.

The people who work in this way are often very gifted and versatile; they are able to perform almost any sort of music. Usually their income from performing is secondary; they often teach as a principal means of livelihood. These musicians become very skillful in mastering new material quickly, because each job is different and there is no routine. Although you often have a greater chance for a bit of solo work, the uncertainties are great and there is absolutely no guarantee that you will have a job from one week or month to the next. It is fairly safe to say that at any given moment, there are more professional musicians looking for work than there are those who have it!

And still another world—that of the younger sound, the pop, rock, folk world. Here there are many possibilities for the performer of genuine talent.

By and large, even the so-called overnight sensations have spent long years practicing, learning, and working toward some specific goal. The search for new sounds, the development of new combinations of instruments, working to develop a repertoire of new material, all take a good deal of talent, a lot of hard training in basic technique and considerable practice and devotion. The basic requirement is a creative spark, the ability to find a new and pleasing effect, a way of communicating something special to the public. The star pop performer has to have a great desire to share his special feelings with others. Without this, he will have a hard time reaching anything close to star proportions. Once again, there is no real substitute for genuine talent, ambition and good luck.

Are there any special education requirements?

Not really. Educational backgrounds vary enormously from high-school diploma, with no formal music education except perhaps instrumental lessons, all the way to college and conservatory degrees. But there is no question that a degree is a considerable advantage to almost everyone who contemplates a career in music. Even a top player may wish at some point in his career to be able to teach classes at a university where such a degree is a prerequisite. The degree may never be used. Then again, it may provide just the right cushion of security to the holder. In any event, it is hard to think of a degree as a handicap. Credentials are always good to have.

Conducting is another highly specialized performing career. Virtually all conductors begin their training as instrumentalists and they almost always have extensive formal training in everything from stick technique to orchestration. Conductors have to know the techniques involved with all the instruments, and must possess a sensitive musical ear and a great instinct for leadership. Most outstanding conductors also possess a prodigious musical memory. The ability to read an entire orchestral score and then be able to recall it in every detail is an invaluable asset. Most of the first-rate conductors have this kind of memory. They can often go to the piano and play a few bars from some particular work even though they have not seen the score for some time.

Becoming a conductor is made even more difficult because there is so little opportunity to work at it on a lower level and hence to gradually move up toward the professional ranks. There is more opportunity to lead vocal groups than instrumental groups. Vocal conductors sometimes move on to conducting orchestras: Robert Shaw, who came to prominence some years ago as a first-rate vocal conductor, has since become the music director of the Atlanta Symphony. And there are others. By and large, the conductor is highly gifted and possesses a broad and deep range of musical abilities and knowledge. It is not a career for the timid or uncertain; the requirements are enormous, and the opportunities are limited.

Composing and arranging are career fields which, almost by definition, require extensive formal training in theory, harmony and orchestration. It is almost impossible to compose as a "primitive," with the instinct and not the skills. Not only is an extraordinary degree of skill necessary but a flair for creative expression is an essential. Today, music seems to be undergoing something of a revolution, along with so many other aspects of our society. Many young composers are seeking new mediums of expression. Technology is increasingly important as electronic devices become more sophisticated and are used more frequently in new works. This has created a new demand on the would-be composer for whom a thorough understanding of the principles of sound and the methods of reproducing sounds with a variety of electronic devices is now almost essential. In addition, there has been a great narrowing of the gap between the "classical" composer and the "pop" composer in recent years. The new breed of composer is seeking ways of uniting old and new and is developing new musical forms and methods of expression. America's Leonard Bernstein is perhaps the outstanding example of a composer equally at home in the world of classical music and that of the Broadway musical. His contributions in both realms mark him as one of a rare breed. Music is being written for and played by computer. Composers such as Milton

Babbitt have helped pioneer this "new music." It has given birth to some very interesting sounds, including the music of Bach transcribed and played electronically. This "Switched-on Bach" has created a whole new dimension which even dyed-in-the-wool classicists find almost irresistible.

There is another small group of composers and arrangers, some of whose members are extraordinarily well paid for their work. They are the ones who compose the jingles, background music and theme music for radio and television. This specialized field is hard to break into, but if one has a feeling for the material, the financial rewards can be quite gratifying.

Somewhere over the horizon are still newer forms and concepts; the breaking apart of the old formal order will be completed by the composers now being trained. It is they who will create the new and valid music of tomorrow. To do so, they must first be thoroughly trained in the basic musical language. Only then can they work with the elements of the language to create new ways of expressing it. There is no shortcut for the composer—he must put in long hours and endure great frustrations.

It is most unfortunate there is so little opportunity for the composer to hear his own works performed by first-rate groups, and to have a proper public hearing of his creations. New works are still the exception on any major symphony program.

It is a rare contemporary composer, indeed, who is able to live on the earnings of his compositions. Therefore, most composers today work as part of the faculty of a relatively large college or university, where they can teach and where there are opportunities to have student performing groups present their new works. Dedicated composers have the insatiable urge to create music and will do so no matter what discouragements are placed in their path.

Another field that is in some ways quite closely allied to composing is *musical arranging*. This is a field the public is ordinarily unaware of, but one which employs many creative and talented musicians. Arranging can be done for band, orchestra, chorus, small ensemble groups, jazz groups, solo instrument or voice and for virtually any combination of instruments and voice. Arrangements can be made for individual performing groups, such as a special arrangement for a performance on television, or for a publisher who will then sell the arrangement to the general public or to school performing groups, etc.

Most of the frequently played music—be it jazz, pop or classical—is constantly being rearranged. Sometimes a new arrangement of an old tune will help it achieve a popularity it never attained originally. An English march tune, "The Colonel Bogey March," became a "standard" after the new arrangement was popularized on the sound track of *The Bridge on the River Kwai*. The special whistle and drum effect the arranger achieved was so "right" that the tune gained world-wide popularity.

Arranging has become particularly important in the pop field. Often a first-rate professional arranger has been brought in to work with a tune written by a well-known performer. It is frequently what the arranger does with the melody that makes the difference between a miss and a big hit. Many folk and pop groups owe much of their success to one special "sound" their arranger created for them.

The arranger is usually relied upon to find a distinctive musical style for a band or dance orchestra, that special sound which readily identifies it even to the casual listener.

A good arranger must have extensive musical skills and the ability to manipulate his materials with ease. He must have a sense of musical taste and style and that special creative impulse which enables him to hear something in his ear and mind before it is set down on paper. Arranging is not simply improvising and then writing it down; it is a distinct and important part of music-making, a special branch of the musical arts.

Although good arrangers are needed, the demand for them is not great. Most of them, therefore, manage to augment their incomes by teaching or playing professionally.

Teaching. Teaching music in the United States today is a career field of major proportions. But, it should be stressed at the outset that while there are many thousands of school music teachers with good positions, this is not, at present, a growing field. Teaching in general, with the single exception of the sciences, has experienced a recession in the United States as population growth has declined and budgets have been cut. Today, there is a surplus of music teachers, and even those well qualified are having difficulty finding permanent positions.

However, there is no doubt that teaching can be a rewarding career for someone who truly enjoys sharing knowledge, and who takes genuine pleasure in watching his students grow. But teaching can become a nightmare for the musicians who go into it simply because that is the only way they can produce an income with their musical knowledge. Perhaps the commandment might be stated as follows: Thou shalt not teach music unless real enjoyment is derived from it. If you violate this commandment you run the grave risk of doing a great injustice to yourself and to your students. Don't forget this point. If you become a teacher, your students will quite literally be at your mercy. If you ever had a teacher you disliked because you knew that teacher disliked teaching, think carefully before you decide to teach.

For those who wish to teach privately, there is no specific training, degree or license required. Many musicians with performing careers do private teaching because it can be an excellent source of supplementary income, and because it is a refreshing challenge that helps them grow and develop as musicians.

The good teacher always learns while teaching. Even the most professional instrumentalist can learn something about the technique of his instrument while watching a beginner struggle with the rudiments of it. One is forced to analyze something in detail to be able to explain it to someone else.

Some private instrumental and vocal music teachers have no formal musical education other than intensive training on their particular instrument. Others have college or conservatory degrees in music.

Some musicians make a full-time career of teaching their instruments and do only incidental performing themselves. Most private music schools do require their teachers to have had some formal music education in addition to professional standing as performers and teaching experience. This formal musical training helps to broaden a musician's overall understanding and makes him a better performer as well as a better teacher. It is therefore highly recommended that virtually everyone interested in either a performing or a teaching career equip himself with a college or music conservatory experience.

Many musicians with a calling to teach choose to

become elementary, junior or senior high-school music teachers. Most states have license requirements for music teachers who wish to work in public education. The major requirement in most states is a bachelor of arts degree in music education. Many high schools will insist that candidates have a master's degree as well. This field covers the teaching of classroom music on all grade levels from kindergarten through high school, the teaching of group instrumental classes and the training and conducting of bands, orchestras and choruses.

Vocal and classroom music teachers are well advised to have a good facility at the piano. Instrumental teachers require a working knowledge of all the instruments they will be dealing with. In a large school system there is a band teacher and another teacher to handle the orchestra. But in a small system, often one teacher must be able to handle both responsibilities. Someone who is expert on the flute but cannot cope with a row of struggling trumpets or clarinets is going to be severely disadvantaged as a band director. But this training is thoroughly covered in a college course leading to a degree in music education.

Teaching on the college level is different in several ways. First, in order to have a reasonably secure career as a college teacher of music one must obtain a doctoral degree. It is true that there are certain exceptions—unusually gifted performers are sometimes able to remain as "artists in residence" and give master classes. But to be part of the hierarchy in a conventional university or college situation, an advanced degree is a must. While it is certainly possible to begin a university teaching career with a master's degree, it is not possible to advance beyond a certain point without going on. The advanced degree does not necessarily make a better professor out of someone, but the "system" will not promote that person without it. Of course there are other elements as well. Excellence in the classroom, conspicuous research or other original work all are significant.

To provide time for research, performing, writing and composing, college teaching usually calls for fewer hours in the classroom. It should be mentioned in passing that, even at this level, teaching is not as secure as it once was. No longer are teachers at the university level automatically offered tenure after a certain number of years. Institutions working with increasingly restricted budgets, staff their faculties more and more with younger, less experienced, and hence less costly, teachers. Still, this discouraging aspect of college-level teaching is not likely to deter those with the urge to devote their working lives to teaching and training young musicians.

There are a variety of special areas also available to the college-level music teacher, some of which are quite attractive and hold enormous potential for both teaching and research. These include the history of music (musicology) and music theory (including harmony, counterpoint, sight-singing, orchestration and the teaching of composition). Additionally there is the teaching of music performance, vocal and instrumental coaching, conducting of bands, orchestras, choruses and so on. These activities are often a great outlet for the teacher who also wants to perform, to be on the stage and at the center of the music-making. This almost unique opportunity which music teachers have is perhaps one of the most attractive aspects of the field.

Another branch of music teaching is musical education, or training music teachers. This is a highly specialized field and requires persons with lively minds, dedicated to the philosophy that the great traditions must be continued while new methods are constantly sought and developed. A good "teacher of teachers" has to have taught successfully himself. He must not only be aware of the latest methods and techniques, but must stay in close contact with the real world of the classroom. The education teachers should be prepared to help lead the dialogue that tells us just what form of music education is important and how we are going to go about providing it. Then they must be ready to deliver. A broad teaching experience, maturity and keen psychological insights all help form a solid music education specialist.

Virtually all these career fields can lead the music educator into administrative work. The management of a large department, the hiring of gifted and inspiring teachers, the development of a healthy atmosphere in which young musicians can grow individually and in groups, a knowledge of what music is right for what student and what group should perform what material—all these are the worries of a school's music supervisor. Good music teachers who have a yen to manage and enjoy seeing the results of their management, can look toward careers as music supervisors. Many major school systems are divided into districts, so a music supervisor often has charge of a large staff of teachers and oversees the musical education and development of a number of young people. The financial rewards for the supervisor are usually higher and the chance to bring one's views into operation on a broad scale can be appealing and satisfying. The drawback of this career is that often the music supervisor loses much of his contact with the students. It is classroom closeness that often provides the music teacher with his most precious moments.

The best way to find out more about each career field is to talk to someone in it. Try your music teacher or band director or music history teacher; often they can provide valuable tips about educational opportunities, practice teaching and the like. Last, it is worth repeating what was said at the beginning of this section. Find out if you really like to teach before you commit yourself too deeply to a career in it. If you and teaching are a mismatch, then discover and admit it early on and avoid the frustration and bitterness that sometimes accompany an unfortunate career choice.

There is at least one music educator's organization which is well worth knowing about. It is the Music Educator's National Conference (MENC), the largest organization of music teachers in the United States. The group holds conventions at the national as well as the state and local levels. It publishes a journal and tries to keep its members informed on new developments in the field. Its purpose is to help improve the quality of music instruction of all kinds. The MENC headquarters are located at 1902 Association Drive, Reston, Virginia 22091. The annual MENC membership dues vary from state to state. The dues cover membership in the national and state organizations and entitle the member to the monthly *Music Educators' Journal* published by MENC, and whatever state publication there may be. The state publications range from the full magazines of the larger states, to newsletters published in some of the smaller states. For an additional minimal fee, a person can become a research member of MENC, entitling him to the organization's quarterly research journal. MENC holds a national conference every other year and six regional conferences on the alternate years. The state organizations hold their own meetings and also sponsor clinics and workshops to provide continuing education in a field where changes are sometimes slow to be effected.

Business careers in music. The opportunities here are virtually limitless both in terms of income and range of activities. They range from managing a world-famous international concert bureau, such as the one which the fabulously successful Sol Hurok directed some years ago, to working as a specialist in sheet-music sales in a store devoted to serving the local musicians and music students. Careers in this area include that of Artists and Repertoire representative. This executive selects the music to be recorded and the artists to record it. The job entails enormous responsibility. A successful A&R executive is one of the superstars of the industry, often drawing a six-figure salary—more than almost everyone in the business except the top artists. Alas, with the public's taste always difficult to assess and the rapid changes in favorites, it is a job with many tensions and a high turnover. In fact, in recent times, the recession has caused major setbacks in the record industry, particularly in the area of classical music. In the United States, there are few if any A&R jobs available in classical recording. Many records are now made abroad where costs are less and technology has developed rapidly.

In the pop music field, major labels have in-house A&R staffs but today, there are also an increasing number of independent "packagers" who develop material and a following of artists which they then sell as packages to the various labels. At best this is a hit-or-miss business with sizable income for the successful record producers, and long days of frustration for the rest.

The recording industry goes through periods of ups and downs, along with the rest of the economy. But there are always new developments. Often a new technology creates a new market. Electronics began to explode with the end of the 1970s and though there have been recent downturns in the record industry, one always hopes that new booms will be forthcoming. The point is that this new technology increases the opportunities for those young people with a knowledge of music and the drive and desire to learn the business.

A less glamorous but certainly more dependable and steady career can be found in the repair of instruments. Tuning pianos and making repairs on string, woodwind and brass instruments employs thousands annually. The ranks of really first-rate tuners and repairmen have thinned as many of the old-timers in the field who came to this country from Europe have retired. However, as the number of players grows, so the demand for such services grows.

Instrument-making is a highly specialized field which requires a great many years in training and apprenticeship. For the person who loves music and considers instruments objects of special beauty in themselves, this can be an intriguing career. Young people with a desire to carve, to mold, to sculpt, to work long hours to perfect a single instrument, can find unusual fulfillment in the exacting task of making instruments by hand. In this career, you must find an expert craftsman and then learn the art, quite literally from scratch. One can also work in one of the many factories which mass-produce musical instruments. Even in mass production, much of the finishing work must be done by hand.

Some instrument-makers also maintain a repair business. This is especially so for string instruments, the principal area for the individual craftsman. It takes many months to make a single good violin. Mass-production techniques have not yet been able to produce anything resembling a Stradivarius. Of course, these handmade instruments are quite costly and often the makers must also work as repairmen in order to develop a reasonable income.

If you have any interest in these areas, one way to test the depth of your interest and to broaden your own perspectives is to try for a job in the local music store or with the local instrument repairman. Working in a store, you will become familiar with the world of music from a different point of view. You will have a chance to see many instruments of varying qualities. You will hear many discussions of teaching and teachers and music and musicians. You will observe every range of taste among the customers. You will probably have a chance to meet and talk to quite a few professional and good amateur musicians.

Listening and asking questions mean learning. You also have a chance to judge your own area of interest. An after-school, weekend or summer job is an ideal way for a young person to gain valuable experience and develop the knowledge from which an intelligent and realistic career choice can later be made.

A final approach to a music career is in the development of part-time opportunities. Music is often pursued as an additional source of income, or as a second career. There are small groups which play for weddings and other social occasions, or pop groups which perform at clubs on weekends. Many pianists find part-time work playing at the rehearsals of a chorus or glee club. Often, the fine singers and instrumentalists performing in churches and synagogues pursue multiple careers. The music librarian for a small orchestra or choral group is frequently a musician in his or her own right who may be pursuing additional training, or someone who has a completely different career. It is not possible to list the many jobs which bring one in contact with the world of music. It is enough to say that the greatest opportunities are open to those with the strongest skills and the best training.

INDEX